C000294806

Rock 'n' Roll Heaven

Rock'n'Roll Heaven

.

Nikki Corvette

Boulevard Books, New York

Photo of Ricky Nelson on page 4 Globe Photos.
Photo of Jim Morrison on page 20 Frank Bez/Globe Photos.
Photo of Andy Gibb on page 34 Dennis Barna/Globe Photos.
Photo of John Lennon on page 52 Globe Photos.
Photo of Karen Carpenter on page 62 Globe Photos.
Photo of Harry Chapin on page 76 Lynn McAfee/Globe Photos.
Photo of Kurt Cobain on page 90 Lisa Rose/Globe Photos.
Photo of Muddy Waters on page 104 Lennox Smillie/Globe Photos.
Photo of Brian Jones on page 114 Jill Gibson/Globe Photos.
Photo of Keith Moon on page 124 Globe Photos.
Photo of Jerry Garcia on page 158 New York Post/Globe Photos.
Author photo courtesy of Robert Matheu.

Rock 'n' Roll Heaven

A Boulevard Book/
published by arrangement with the author.

PRINTING HISTORY
Boulevard trade paperback edition/June 1997

All rights reserved.
Copyright © 1997 by Nikki Corvette.
This book may not be reproduced in whole
or in part, by mimeograph or any other means,
without permission. For information address:
The Berkley Publishing Group, 200 Madison Avenue,
New York, New York 10016.

Book design by Richard Oriolo

The Putnam Berkley World Wide Web site address is
http://www.berkley.com

ISBN: 0-57297-167-3

BOULEVARD
Boulevard Books are published by The Berkley Publishing Group,
200 Madison Avenue, New York, New York 10016.
BOULEVARD and its logo are trademarks
belonging to Berkley Publishing Corporation.

PRINTED IN THE UNITED STATES OF AMERICA

10 9 8 7 6 5 4 3 2 1

Contents

·

4. Murder, She Wrote

Sam Cooke/54   Marvin Gaye/56   John Lennon/59

·

5. Morbid Maladies

Karen Carpenter/64   Eric Carr/66   Woody Guthrie/69

Freddie Mercury/71   Frank Zappa/73

·

6. Life in the Fast Lane

Jesse Belvin/78   Marc Bolan/79   Cliff Burton/81   Harry Chapin/82

Eddie Cochran/84   Pete De Freitas/86   Dave Prater/87

·

7. Kamikazes

Kurt Cobain/92   Ian Curtis/95   Terry Kath/97   Richard Manuel/98   Del Shannon/101

·

8. Slow Fade

Tom Fogerty/106   Alan Freed/108   Muddy Waters/109

·

9. Odd Outtakes

·

10. The Longest Chapter

·

11. Together Beyond the Grave

Rock 'n' Roll was, is, and always will be a major part of my life. This book is dedicated to the music and everyone who makes it, especially the ones we've lost.

Introduction

On December 6, 1995, the *New York Post* declared that Michael Jackson was "fifteen minutes from death." He had collapsed on the stage of the Beacon Theater and was rushed to the hospital where he was treated for dehydration and an overstressed heart.

Michael Jackson's condition received especially wide exposure because he fell ill just hours before the broadcast of the *Billboard Music Awards*. The show was aired on Fox Television, a network which is just one piece of Rupert Murdoch's multimedia empire that includes newspapers, publishing houses, film studios, and television networks around the world. In many ways, the *Billboard* show exemplified the current state of music and could give one pause to ask the central question—is rock 'n' roll dead?

Making music has become a complicated and bureaucratic endeavor involving video, advertising, and publicity campaigns—and, of course, millions of dollars. The buying and selling of the arts favors the large and destroys the small, and in order to succeed, most artists must play by a set of strict commercial rules. The term rock 'n' roll now includes a variety of sub-genres—punk, metal, alternative, dance, pop—that indicate the music industry's ability to please everyone.

But before we sign rock 'n' roll's death certificate, let's take a look at the *Billboard* top forty. At the airing of the *Music Awards*, the number one spot on the pop chart was held by . . . the Beatles. Thirty years after the Beatles kicked off the British Invasion and fifteen years after the death of John Lennon, the Beatles were back. Their new single, "Free as a Bird," included the work of the three surviving Beatles as well as vocals from the dearly departed, courtesy of technology.

There is no doubt that rock 'n' roll has changed since the Beatles crossed the Atlantic.

On August 1, 1981, less than a year after Lennon's death, MTV hit the airwaves, amalgamating radio, television, and recorded music to an unprecedented extent. MTV spawned a generation of artists who concerned themselves as much with their "look" as with their sound, and soon the visual performance rivaled the music in importance. Although this emphasis created countless critics of MTV, it also created the dance wonders of Janet Jackson, Paula Abdul, and Madonna.

The rise of these powerful women heralded also a chipping away at the gender barrier that had encased rock 'n' roll for so long. Although most of the names in this book are male, the dance, pop, and R&B queens have given the boys a run for their money. In fact, the 1995 Billboard Artist of the Year was TLC, a tough young trio of black women who have sold more records than any other female group in the history of rock 'n' roll.

Although the business, the technology, and the gender aspects of rock 'n' roll may have changed, the rock 'n' roll lifestyle has remained the same. Rock stars, living each day to the extreme, have retained their larger-than-life status. We follow their every move—each triumph and each mishap. This book chronicles the final mishaps of many of our favorites. Many of the stars included in this book "struck it rich" after they were dead, and some of the fans of these post-humous hits may not have even known that the artists were dead. As the Beatles showed us, rock 'n' roll can resurrect a human being in the ears of millions. But, although mortal musicians can create timeless tunes, the passing of these rockers serves as a reminder of their humanity.

The book's chapters correspond to the various ways that contributors to the canon of rock 'n' roll bid farewell to this world. It details the underbelly of a way of life—fast cars, private planes, and over-the-top risks—that will always characterize the rock 'n' roll persona. It is clear that drugs top the charts as the number one killer, and one can only imagine the panoply of musical geniuses that would be with us today if heroin had never been discovered. Then again, one cannot imagine rock 'n' roll music without the drug culture.

Not all of our rockers had deaths as large as their lives. Some of them slipped from life, slowly or painfully or quietly, and died in obscurity long after their glory days had faded. Some were taken from us before they reached or even approached their potential. None passed, however, without leaving at least a few saddened fans and some small hole in the quilt of rock 'n' roll. So rock 'n' roll is not dead: the music will live on in CDs, music videos, hearts and minds, and the musicians will rock on together in the jam session in the sky that we call . . . *Rock 'n' roll Heaven.*

Chapter 1

.

Crash Landings

Big Bopper, Buddy Holly, Ritchie Valens

T he losses of Buddy Holly, Ritchie Valens, and J. P. (The Big Bopper) Richardson were in many ways the first true rock 'n' roll deaths. These pioneers of rock perished in a plane crash in 1959, and Don McLean's 1971 hit "American Pie" summed up the affair as "the day the music died."

Charles Hardin Holly (originally Holley) was born in Lubbock, Texas, on September 7, 1936. As a young boy, Buddy learned to play the piano, violin, and guitar, and when he was thirteen, he and his friend Bob Montgomery created a western-bop duo called Buddy and Bob. They started playing shows and soon had their own radio program on KDAV, Lubbock. Buddy and Bob signed with Decca Records and released several singles, with little success. Decca refused to release their last single, "That'll Be The Day," and the contract was terminated.

In early 1957, Buddy put together a new band, the Crickets, and started recording in Clovis, New Mexico, with producer Norman Petty. Buddy Holly and the Crickets experimented with many techniques that would become standards of future rock 'n' roll, including overdubs and double tracking in the studio, writing their own material, and combining different musical styles. In addition, the Crickets' lineup of two guitars, a bass, and drums became the basic rock 'n' roll band that has persisted to the present day.

With Norman Petty as manager and producer, the Crickets signed with Brunswick Records; Buddy simultaneously signed a solo deal with Coral. "That'll Be The Day" was the Crickets' first release, in May of 1957. Backed by a national tour, "That'll Be The Day" made it to number three on the charts. The next year, the Crickets as a band and Buddy on his own both had numerous hits, including "Peggy Sue," "Maybe Baby," "Rave On," "Everyday," and "Oh Boy."

In October 1958, Buddy inexplicably split from

the group and dumped Petty. The band dissolved on friendly terms, but the legal and financial problems that followed were hard on Buddy. He didn't want to leave his pregnant wife Maria, but money was tight and a reluctant Buddy joined the "Winter Dance Party Tour" early in 1959.

Jiles Perry Richardson was born in Sabine, Texas, on October 24, 1930. As a young boy, he shortened his name to J. P. and dubbed himself "Big Bopper" in reference to his large size. J. P.'s love of music was already evident in high school: he wrote songs, joined a band, and worked as a disc jockey.

After high school, J. P. spent several years in the U.S. Army before returning home to Beaumont, Texas. He reclaimed his DJ position at K-TRM Radio, the same job he had had in high school. While working there he broke the world record for nonstop broadcasting by being on the air continuously for five days, two hours, and eight minutes. Between marathon DJ shifts, J. P. began to sing and write songs in the hopes of securing a record deal. The Big Bopper hit the big time in August of 1958 when his original song, "Chantilly Lace," was released by Mercury Records and sold over a million copies. Within a short period of time, he followed his debut with another hit, "Big Bopper's Wedding." With two hits under his belt, J. P. took a leave of absence from K-TRM to join the "Winter Dance Party Tour" in 1959.

*   *   *

Ritchie Valens will go down in history as one of the first Latino pop stars. He was born Richard Valenzuela on May 13, 1941, in Pacoima, California. The Valenzuelas were a musical family and Ritchie's father's Latin guitar filled the house with Mexican music. Ritchie started singing and playing acoustic Spanish guitar when he was very young and built his first electric guitar while he was attending Pacoima Junior High School. He used this guitar until he saved enough money to buy a Fender Stratocaster. In 1957, Ritchie started his own band, the Silhouettes, one of the first Mexican rock bands to hit the U.S. His mother scraped together enough money to rent a hall, and the family held a dance with Ritchie's band as the entertainment. The dance was so successful that they started to hold them regularly until Ritchie was discovered by Bob Keene of Del-Fi Records.

In 1958, Richard Valenzuela became Ritchie Valens for his mildly successful Del-Fi debut, "Come On, Let's Go." Several months later he started his first tour, steadily gaining momentum with well received concerts on the West Coast and several guest spots on *American Bandstand*.

Back in Los Angeles, Ritchie recorded his second single, "Donna," a love song he wrote for his high school sweetheart, Donna Ludwig. The B-side was an updated version of a traditional Mexican folk song, "La Bamba." It became a double-sided hit as both songs climbed the charts. Then, in January of 1959, a thrilled Ritchie joined his first major national tour, the "Winter Dance Party Tour."

*   *   *

The Winter Dance Party was a difficult tour—there were bus problems, overcrowding, poor weather, and a jam-packed schedule. Buddy Holly wanted to avoid the unpleasantness, and after the Surf City Ballroom show in Clear Lake, Iowa, he chartered a plane to take him to the next engagement. Buddy invited Ritchie Valens and Waylon Jennings to join him, but it was J. P. and not Jennings who ended up on the plane. The tour was especially rough on the Big Bopper, whose generous dimensions made the cramped bus practically unbearable. When he heard that Holly had chartered a plane, he convinced Waylon Jennings to give up his seat.

It was snowing and windy when Buddy Holly, Ritchie Valens, J. P. Richardson, and pilot Roger Peterson left the Mason City airport for Fargo, North Dakota. The single-engine Beechcraft Bonanza took off in the wee hours of February 3, 1959. It crashed into an empty field shortly after takeoff. There were no survivors.

Buddy Holly's funeral was held on January 27, 1959, at the Tabernacle Baptist Church, in Lubbock. Although he was only twenty-two at the time of his death, one thousand people gathered to pay their final respects. "It Doesn't Matter Anymore" was one of Buddy's last recordings, and it became a major hit when it was released several months after his death. The memorial album, *The Buddy Holly Story*, reached gold status, and the film by the same name was a hit in 1978. Buddy is remembered in many ways—his songs are heavily covered and there is an annual celebration held in Lubbock, which is also home to a statue in his honor.

J. P. Richardson was buried at Forest Lawn Memorial Park in Beaumont, Texas. Although the Big Bopper had no posthumous releases of his own, he did have one final success. "Running Bear," a song he had written for his friend Johnny Preston, became a hit the year after J. P.'s death.

Ritchie Valens was buried at the San Fernando Mission cemetery in San Fernando, California. When Ritchie died at the age of seventeen, his career had spanned only a few short years, but his songs have become rock classics. His music lives on, as seen in 1987 with the hit movie *La Bamba*, which was based on his life. Released almost thirty years after his death, the film introduced Ritchie and his music to a brand-new generation. On May 11, 1990, Ritchie Valens became the first Latino pop star to receive a star on the Hollywood Walk of Fame.

Patsy Cline

Patsy Cline was one of the first female country singers to cross over into the pop music world. Although at the time many considered her crazy, today, artists of many different musical backgrounds strive to copy her unique style.

Patsy Cline was born Virginia Patterson Hensley on September 8, 1932, in Winchester, Virginia. Patsy started small—singing covers on a local radio station and in clubs before she was discovered by Fourstar Records. In June of 1955, Patsy appeared at Nashville's Grand Ole Opry and soon became a regular on Jimmy Dean's "Town and Country Jamboree." These performances led in turn to a television appearance on *Arthur Godfrey's Talent Scouts* in 1957. The judges were blown away by Patsy's rendition of "Walkin' After Midnight," and she won the contest and secured a record deal with Decca.

"Walkin' After Midnight," Patsy's first release on the Decca label, made it to number three on the country charts and number twelve on the pop charts. Patsy soon returned to the Grand Ole Opry, but she did not have another hit until "I Fall To Pieces" hit the charts in 1961. In June of '61, Patsy's career temporarily fell to pieces after a near-fatal car accident in Tennessee. While still on crutches, Patsy recorded Willie Nelson's song "Crazy"—it became her greatest hit.

On March 5, 1963, Patsy performed in a benefits concert for the widow of DJ Cactus Jack Call. Patsy's manager, Randy Hughes, was to fly Patsy and several other country singers home in a single engine Piper Comanche. At approximately 6:00 P.M., they gassed up in Dyersburg, Tennessee, and headed for Nashville. They never made it home. The plane crashed near Camden, Tennessee, and Patsy, her manager, and two other country stars— Hawkshaw Hawkins and Country Copas—were killed instantly.

Over 25,000 fans attended Patsy Cline's Nashville funeral. She is buried at the Shenandoah Memorial Park in Winchester, Virginia.

Jim Croce

Jim Croce was a common man with an uncommon talent for making music. His easy, direct manner made him a crowd favorite, and his refreshing, earnest sound makes him a record listener's friend. Although by a cruel twist of fate he is not with us today, he still has a unique niche in the annals of rock 'n' roll.

Jim Croce was born in Philadelphia on January 10, 1943, and was playing the accordion at the age of six. He grew up with a love of music and learned to play the twelve-string guitar while in college at Villanova University. At Villanova, Croce was a psychology major and a DJ on the school radio station, spinning the blues and folk hits. He graduated in 1965, and after a brief foray into the coffeehouse music scene he sold his guitars and settled on a Pennsylvania farm with his wife Ingrid. Though latent, Croce's musical aspirations did not die, and he kept his voice warmed up with occasional work on television commercials. Jim's day job, driving construction trucks, gave him time to write songs in his head, and soon he decided to take another crack at professional music.

In 1973, Jim Croce returned to the coffeehouse and college campus circuit, playing and singing his fresh originals to enthusiastic audiences. He mixed folk, blues, and pop influences and developed a unique style that was accessible to fans from all walks of life. Encouraged by his live successes, Croce recorded an album, *You Don't Mess Around With Jim*. His songs were beginning to pop up on radio stations across the country when Jim's life and times came to a tragic halt. On the way to a show on September 20, 1973, Jim's chartered plane crashed in Natchitoches, Louisiana, and Croce was killed.

Jim's legacy, his music, had been preserved on his album, the sales of which tripled after his death. By February of 1974, the album had sold over a million copies and reached the coveted number one spot of the Billboard chart. Two tracks from the LP made the singles charts; the title track, "Time in a Bottle," and "Operator" were all hits in their own rights and confirmed the versatility and depth of Croce's talent. Jim had been in the midst of recording a second album when he died, and three of the songs from *I Got a Name* continued the posthumous success. "I Got a Name" was released as a single in 1973, and "I'll Have to Say I Love You in a Song" and "Working at the Carwash Blues" were released to an adoring public in 1974. The album itself went gold, as did two other posthumous compilations, *Life and Times* and later, *Photographs and Memories*. Early in 1974, *I Got a Name* held the number two spot on the chart while *Life and Times* sat at number twenty-three. Looking at such success, one can only wonder how far Jim Croce could have gone if he had taken the train.

Rick Nelson

Rick Nelson's career will perhaps always be remembered for the years of his youth spent on the *Adventures of Ozzie and Harriet* show. This focus is perhaps unfair, as later in his career Rick blossomed into an innovative rock 'n' roller.

Ricky Nelson was born Eric Hillard in Teaneck, New Jersey, on May 8, 1940. As part of a show business family, he got started when just eight years old, playing himself on his parents' radio show, *The Adventures of Ozzie and Harriet*. The show moved to television in 1952 and millions of viewers watched each week. Ricky literally grew up before their eyes during the show's fourteen-year run.

Fact and fantasy merged together on TV in 1957 when Ricky formed a band and started to sing on the show. In May 1957, Verve Records released his first single, "A Teenager's Romance/ I'm Walking," a double-sided hit which went gold after Ricky performed both songs on the show. He repeated this success several months later with "Be-Bop Baby," the first record on his new label, Imperial. A pattern soon emerged as Ricky continued to introduce his new songs on the television show, and this strategy led to an impressive string of hits, including "Poor Little Fool," "It's Late," "Hello Mary Lou," and "Travelin' Man."

Ricky wanted to be more than a teen idol, and

he started the transformation to a more mature image by officially changing his name to Rick on his twenty-first birthday. Although Rick signed a big new contract with Decca, his career began to decline with the end of "Ozzie and Harriet" and the arrival of the British Invasion. Soon Rick was reduced to playing nightclubs and rock 'n' roll revival shows instead of major concerts, but this downscaling had a positive side as it led to Rick's exploration of different musical directions.

Rick debuted his new sound in 1966 with the release of *Bright Lights, Country Music*, but while the critics loved it, sales were poor. He persevered and continued to produce critically acclaimed and publicly ignored work. His creations in this era placed Rick firmly as one of the pioneers in the country-rock genre.

In 1969, Rick Nelson put together a band that would come to be known as the Stone Canyon Band. Their version of Bob Dylan's song "She Belongs to Me" finally put Nelson back on the charts after a five-year hiatus. Two years later the band was struggling for recognition and was again reduced to playing oldies shows. Rick was crushed when a Madison Square Garden audience booed his new material and screamed for his old hits. He turned this trauma into a triumph, however, by writing a song about the incident. The song, "Garden Party," became Rick's first gold record in ten years. Rick charted several more records, but he produced nothing that could approach his earlier fame. Rick continued to tour and record with the band, supplementing his musical career with occasional acting jobs throughout the seventies and eighties.

On Tuesday, December 31, 1985, Rick chartered a DC3 to fly the band from Guntersville, Alabama, to a New Year's Eve show in Dallas, Texas. They never made it to the show—the plane caught fire in midair and exploded after crash-landing near DeKalb, Texas. Although no official cause was found for the fire, there were rumors in the entertainment industry that the fire was caused by members of the band freebasing cocaine. The entire Stone Canyon Band died in the crash, including Rick, Helen Blair (his fiancée), Clark Russell (the sound engineer), Bobby Neal (guitar), Rick Intveld (drums), Patrick Woodward (bass), and Andy Chapin (steel guitar). Both the pilot and the copilot survived.

Rick Nelson's memorial service was held on January 6, 1985, at the Church of the Hills, Forest Lawn Memorial Park in Burbank, California.

Otis Redding

The respect with which rock 'n' rollers utter the name of Otis Redding is staggering. In his short life he made countless contributions—in songwriting as well as performing and recording—to the sound of soul. We can only imagine the fruits that his labors would have born had the weatherman predicted the heavy fog.

Otis Redding was born on September 9, 1941, in Dawson, Georgia. He was raised in Macon City, the son of a Baptist minister. At an early age he joined the church choir where he was introduced to gospel music, his first influence. However, several years later he discovered Little Richard and R&B, which led to a change in musical direction.

Although Otis recorded his first single, "Shout Bamalama," in 1960 for the Bethlehem label, his real break into the music business was working as a driver/backup singer for R&B band Johnny Jenkins and the Pinetoppers. In 1962, Otis drove Johnny Jenkins to Memphis to record for a new label, Stax, and when there was time left at the end, he convinced them to let him sing. He did an original, "These Arms of Mine," which impressed the record executives enough to sign him to Stax's Volt label. Otis had a string of hits on the R&B charts, many of which he wrote himself, including "Mr. Pitiful" (1965), "I've Been Loving You Too Long" (1965), and "Fa-Fa-Fa-Fa-Fa" (1966).

Otis helped several other musical careers in different ways. He wrote "Respect," which sent Aretha Franklin on her way to success; recorded a duet album with Carla Thomas, featuring the hit "Tramp"; and produced a number one hit, "Sweet Soul Music," for his protégé, Arthur Conley.

Otis toured extensively but was largely unknown to white audiences until his appearance at the Monterey Pop Festival, where his electrifying performance won over the crowd. This opened up a whole new audience for him and helped him cross over to the pop charts.

Then, just as his career was taking off, it crashed. On Sunday, December 10, 1967, Redding's new twin-engine Beechcraft plane left Cleveland, Ohio, to fly him and his backup band

The Bar-Kays to their next show. In heavy fog, the plane crashed into freezing Lake Monona, near Madison, Wisconsin, just four miles from their destination. Otis Redding was only twenty-six years old when he died along with four members of his band. Jimmy King, Phalin Jones, and Carl Cunningham were eighteen, and Ron Caldwell was nineteen when they died. Ben Cauley was the sole survivor, though he was scarred by the experience—he heard his band mates calling for help but could not reach them.

Almost 5,000 people showed up at the memorial service held for Otis in the Macon City Auditorium. James Brown and Wilson Pickett were among the high profile mourners, and the pallbearers were Percy Sledge, Sam Moore, Joe Tex, Solomon Burke, Joe Simon, Johnnie Taylor, and Don Covay; Booker T. played the organ. Otis was buried at Roundoak, a private cemetery on his family's land just outside Macon, Georgia. The Otis Redding Memorial Bridge, spanning the Ocumelgee River, was dedicated in 1974.

Ironically, Otis Redding's biggest hit was released after his death; "(Sittin' on) the Dock of the Bay" sold over a million copies. This gold record stands as yet another testament to the talent and unfulfilled potential that was Otis Redding.

Randy Rhoads

At the time of his death, quick-fingered Randy Rhoads was on his way to becoming one of the top guitarists in the hard-edged rock 'n' roll scene. Unfortunately, an ill-fated joyride cut his life short. One can only imagine, with twenty more mad years with Ozzy Osbourne, what kind of a diary Rhoads could have written.

Randy was born on December 6, 1956, and was raised in southern California. His early interest in music was natural since his mother ran a music school and encouraged him when he started to play the guitar at the age of seven.

Ten years later, in 1975, Randy Rhoads formed the band Quiet Riot with singer Kevin DuBrow. Based in Los Angeles, they were part of the early heavy metal scene where they soon built a strong following. Although the American record companies were not interested in their sound, Quiet Riot signed with the Japanese Sony/CBS label in 1977 and released their eponymous debut album later that same year. They followed this debut with *Quiet Riot II* and a single, "Slick Black Cadillac," in 1978. All three offerings did well in Japan and Los Angeles but failed to propel the band into the mainstream. The band was discouraged by the narrow scope of their success, and in 1980 Quiet Riot called it quits.

Several months later, Randy's luck took a turn when he joined Ozzy Osbourne's new band, the Blizzard of Ozz. The band had a contract with Jet Records and their debut album eventually went platinum. The band spent the next year touring and recording; their second album, *Diary of a Madman*, also achieved platinum status. On January of 1982, The Blizzard of Ozz embarked on a U.S. tour in support of their second album, and Randy felt that he had finally arrived.

On March 19, 1982, the band took a day off in Orlando, Florida. Andrew Aycock, the tour driver and pilot, decided to have a little fun and took Randy and Rachel Youngblood (Ozzy's hairdresser) for a ride in the band's plane. They "buzzed" the tour bus, then buzzed it again and again. On the last pass, Andrew brought the plane too close and the tip of the wing hit the bus. Aycock lost control and the plane crashed. Although no one on the bus was injured, the three joyriders in the plane were killed. Randy Rhoads was twenty-five years old. He is buried at the Mountain View Cemetery in San Bernardino, California.

In May 1987, Ozzy Osbourne released the album *Tribute* and dedicated it to Randy Rhoads. *Tribute* contained live recordings from 1981 and 1982 and was a showcase of Randy's guitar virtuosity. The album's success, five years after his death, is evidence of Randy's impact as a guitar player and assures his place in musical history.

Stevie Ray Vaughan

Rock 'n' roll is in many ways a child of the blues, and no one fused the two quite like Stevie Ray Vaughan. He firmly established himself in the seventies and eighties as one of the masters of the guitar, playing with many big commercial names but always maintaining his independence and dedication to the art.

Stevie Ray Vaughan was born in 1956 in Dallas, Texas. Although his father worked at an asbestos plant and the Vaughans lived a simple life, their home was always filled with music. Stevie's older brother Jimmy was addicted to the guitar and went on to found the Fabulous Thunderbirds. Following Jimmy's lead, Stevie started playing the guitar at the age of seven and began performing in local clubs when he was fourteen. Being more interested in his guitar than his schoolwork, Stevie dropped out of high school two years later and decided to pursue a career in music. Austin was where the action—and Jimmy—was, and so young Stevie went there in search of his fate.

He found several bands that gave him experience and exposure—the Nightcrawlers, the Cobras, and Triple Threat. He needed the chance to stretch his blues wings, to try out the things that he had heard on his B. B. King, Albert Collins, and Buddy Guy albums. In an interview with *Guitar Player*, Vaughan's band mate from the Cobras remembered Stevie: ''Actually, he was just too much of a guitar player for a band like that [the Cobras]. He'd do a solo and play all the guts out of a song.'' From the Cobras, Vaughan went on to join Triple Threat, a band with five lead vocalists. Vaughan soon outgrew Triple Threat as well and departed, with fellow Triple Threat member Lou Ann Barton, to form his own band, Double Trouble. Barton soon left to pursue a solo career, but Vaughan was joined by bassist Tommy Shannon and drummer Chris ''Whipper'' Layton, and the group took off. Double Trouble made a name for itself for its intense, unique fusion of blues, R&B, and rock.

The Double Trouble word spread far and wide, and in 1982 the Rolling Stones invited the group to play in New York at the Danceteria club. They also attracted the attention of producer Jerry Wexler, who finagled them a spot in the Montreux Jazz Festival, a remarkable feat for an unrecorded band. In the Montreux audience was David Bowie, who was floored by Vaughan's talent and asked him to play on his next album and tour. *Let's Dance* turned out to be one of David Bowie's most successful albums and gave Vaughan a broad new exposure. The texture of his jazzlike improvisations and lightning fast style put the album a cut above the standard fare of the day, and the partnership seemed beneficial to Stevie and David. Two days before departure, however, Vaughan backed out of the tour, to Bowie's disappointment but understanding. Bowie told *Guitar World*, "Stevie didn't make it to the touring stage with us last year because he had his own illustrious career to get on with, and he did very well, indeed."

Stevie continued down the path of independence, and success, for the rest of his life. Jackson Browne recognized Vaughan's brilliance and offered him the use of his recording studio, free of charge. The results of the sessions were snatched up by renowned producer John Hammond and released under the Epic label in 1983 as *Texas Flood*. The album exhibited the range and depth of Vaughan's extraordinary ability, from the driving rhythm of "Love Struck Boy" to the rolling melodies of "Lenny."

Jimmy Vaughan joined his big little brother and Double Trouble on the next album, *Couldn't Stand the Weather*, and this second offering showed even more versatility than the first. The sound ranged from the jazzy "Stang's Swang" to the exquisite and faithful cover of Hendrix's "Voodoo Chile (Slight Return)." Vaughan's gift was indisputable, and for the second year in a row, he won the *Guitar Player* readers' poll for the Best Electric Blues Guitarist. Vaughan won praise also from one of his first idols, Lonnie Mack, and Stevie began work on Mack's comeback album in 1985. The praise kept coming, and in 1985 Vaughan garnered both the *Guitar Player* award, for the third time, and the W. C. Handy Blues Foundation's Blues Entertainer of the Year Award (becoming the first white man to win the latter).

Stevie Ray Vaughan's loyal Double Trouble expanded in 1986 to include Reese Wyans on keyboards and Joe Sublett on sax. The new group headed back to the studio to record their next album, *Soul to Soul*, which highlighted Stevie Ray's ever-increasing innovation and a fuller sound from the enlarged band. Hendrix covers like "Come On" exhibited Vaughan's virtuosity while the originals like "Say What!" revealed his considerable songwriting talents. The picture was not, however, entirely rosy. In a constant effort to keep up with his own image, Stevie Ray turned to cocaine and heavy drinking. The habits caught up with him on the *Soul to Soul* tour when Vaughan collapsed on a London stage. Vaughan saw the writing on the wall and checked himself into the Marietta Clinic. His fourth album, *Live Alive!*, was released while he was in rehab, and though some denied that it was up to his normal caliber, the album was nominated for a Grammy. Stevie finished off 1986 the same way he had finished off the last three years, by winning *Guitar Player's* Electric Blues Player of the Year.

Through the next five years, Stevie Ray Vaughan continued creating music with the aggressiveness and spirit that made him famous. In 1989, he released *In Step*, which included not only original tracks of breathtakingly high quality, but also a candid and heartfelt narrative about his battles with drugs and alcohol. In 1990, Stevie Ray embarked on a tour with Jeff Beck and recorded a duo album with brother Jimmy. He continued to play shows of all sizes—above all else, Stevie Ray Vaughan loved to perform.

It was fitting, then, that performing would be Stevie Ray's last memory. On August 27, 1990, Vaughan wrapped up a stellar impromptu jam with two of his most esteemed colleagues, Eric Clapton and Robert Cray. After the show, Stevie Ray Vaughan boarded his private helicopter to return home from East Troy, Wisconsin. He never made it home. The helicopter crashed soon after takeoff and Stevie Ray Vaughan was killed. As the music world mourned the loss, brother Jimmy went to work compiling a posthumous collection of Stevie's work, *The Sky Is Crying*. The final album came out in 1991 and joined its predecessors as a testament to the greatness of Stevie Ray Vaughan.

Chapter 2

.

Off the Wagon

John Bonham

John Bonham, Led Zeppelin's infamous drummer, never failed to create a scene—on stage or off. This same restless spirit set fire to his drumsticks and, eventually, sent him up the stairway to heaven.

Born in Redditch, Worcestershire, England, on May 31, 1948, John Henry Bonham grew up in Kidderminster, a rural suburb of Birmingham. John, the son of a carpenter, began his musical career imitating his father by pounding on his mother's pots and pans. When John was ten, his mother bought him his first snare drum set, and five years later John's father gave him a full set of used, slightly rusted drums. John was sixteen when he left school to work for his father during the day and play music at night. In that first year, he drummed for Terry Webb and the Spiders, the Nicky James Movement, and A Way of Life.

When John turned seventeen, he married his girlfriend Pat and began to play with a new local group called the Crawling King Snakes. The lead singer of the Snakes, Robert Plant, became attached to the young drummer. When Plant went solo, Bonham joined him on his third CBS single, "Long Time Comin'/I've Got A Secret." Soon they were playing together in an R&B group called Band of Joy. Breaking out of Birmingham and into the London club scene, the band backed up American singer Tim Rose before they split up in the spring of 1968. After the breakup, John bounced back just like "Bonzo," the amiable cartoon character for whom he was nicknamed. He spent the next few months on the club circuit, backing the likes of Joe Cocker and Chris Farlowe.

Meanwhile, in July of 1968, the Yardbirds also broke up, leaving guitarist Jimmy Page to fulfill a contract for ten concerts in Scandinavia. Page added John Paul Jones on bass/keyboards, but he did not have a singer or a drummer. As replacements, Page found Plant who in turn suggested his old friend John Bonham to complete the lineup.

The group played together for the first time a few days after the lineup had been set, and right from the start all four members agreed that it felt like magic. After quickly learning a number of American R&B and blues classics, the New Yardbirds left for Copenhagen on September 14, 1968. Following a successful tour, the band returned to London in October and headed to the studio. With Jimmy Page as the producer, the group's first album was completed in two weeks, using only thirty hours of studio time. The result was a groundbreaking mix of power chords, thundering rhythm, and slicing, blues-tinged vocals that formed the definitive sound of a new heavy metal.

The band decided on the name Led Zeppelin, based on a joking remark made by Keith Moon of The Who, who said that the group would go down like a lead zeppelin. Although they did several more shows as the New Yardbirds to fulfill contract obligations, on October 15, 1968, Led Zeppelin officially made their live debut at Surrey University. In the meantime, their manager Peter Grant took their tapes to New York, and a month later Led Zeppelin became the first white rock band to be signed by Atlantic Records. Their contract included a $200,000 advance, which at that time was the largest advance ever to be paid a musician. In addition, Led Zeppelin was given complete artistic autonomy—an almost unheard-of freedom. Their Ameri-

can debut came in the form of an unannounced show in Denver followed by an official concert in Boston, opening for Vanilla Fudge and the MC5.

Although Led Zeppelin's album had not yet been released, advance copies were sent to radio stations throughout the country, preparing the American concert audience for the Zeppelin sound. Although the band initially lost money on the early release, the exposure they received turned out to be priceless compensation. In January 1969, the eponymous debut album hit the record stores and was met with an enthusiastic response. The UK received the album in March, but after the American triumph, Led Zeppelin's return to London was a bit of a letdown. The band toured England for two months and then headed back to the U.S. for a second tour. In the course of this successful tour, Led Zeppelin's album climbed into the American top ten. Their follow-up album, *Led Zeppelin II*, hit number one on both sides of the Atlantic and stayed on the American charts for ninety-eight weeks.

In October of 1969, the band played the first rock concert at New York's Carnegie Hall since a riotous Rolling Stones show four years earlier had resulted in a ban. Later in 1969, Zeppelin's harsh distorted blues number, "Whole Lotta Love," was taken from their album and released as a single without the band's permission—it charted at number four. When "Stairway to Heaven" from *Led Zeppelin IV* hit the stores in November 1971, Led Zeppelin was assured of rock immortality.

The rest of the decade was an impressively un-varying routine of touring and recording, yielding three number one albums, *Houses of the Holy*, *Physical Graffiti*, and *Presence*. In 1976, the band released the documentary concert film *The Song Remains the Same*.

"Bonzo" played the drums with thundering passion, and his lengthy solos were often the high points of Led Zeppelin shows. His performances were brutal—he often played without sticks, beating the drums with his hands. In all areas of life, John was a slave to excess, and he drank and partied as hard as he played the drums. He did not handle alcohol well, and the sight of Bonzo passed out at the side of a room was quite commonplace. When he managed to remain conscious, John's antics were often violent and antisocial; in 1977 Bonzo was arrested for beating up a security guard in Oakland, California. Numerous other incidents, famous, infamous, and perverse, frequently catapulted Bonham into the entertainment industry's gossip mill.

On September 24, 1980, Led Zeppelin planned to rehearse at Jimmy Page's house in Windsor. John stopped at a pub on the way and downed four screwdrivers. At Page's, he continued to drink vodka throughout the rehearsal, and when he passed out on the couch sometime after midnight, no one thought anything of it. Roadies carried him off to bed, turning him on his side for safety, as they had dozens of times before, but this time would turn out to be the last. At 1:45 the next afternoon, John Bonham was discovered dead in his bed. The official cause of death was alcohol poisoning from the more than forty shots of vodka that he had consumed in a twelve-hour period, but he had also choked on his vomit in his sleep.

Bonzo was cremated and services were held October 10 at the Rushock Parish Church near his farm. In December, the band released a statement to the press:

> We wish it to be known that the loss of our dear friend and the deep respect we have for his family, together with a sense of undivided harmony felt by ourselves and our manager, have led us to decide that we could not continue as we were.

Led Zeppelin had died with Bonzo.

Steve Clark

Def Leppard rode in on the "new wave" of British heavy metal at the close of the 1970's and saw their version of metal rise to the top of the rock 'n' roll mainstream. More melodic and palatable than the older, harder heavy metal, the music of Def Leppard was characterized by youth and an emphasis on visual effects. They have often been put in the category of "lite" metal, but that label did not stop them from offering enough raunch to win them a place on Tipper Gore's list of the "filthy fifteen."

Steve Clark was born on April 23, 1960, in Hillsborough, South Yorkshire. At the age of seventeen, Clark caught wind of a new metal band starting up in nearby Sheffield. The band had been started when two of Clark's college friends, Pete Willis and Joe Elliot, teamed up with bassist Rick Savage to form Atomic Mass. Vocalist Elliot suggested a new name, Deaf Leopard, and the title mutated. Steve Clark wanted to join Willis on guitar, and the band agreed to listen to him play. Clark blew them away with his rendition of the guitar solo from Lynyrd Skynyrd's "Freebird," and Def Leppard expanded by one. It expanded once again when Rick Allen came aboard as the permanent drummer. At fifteen, Allen was the youngest member of the band, but even Elliot, the oldest, was only nineteen at the time.

Def Leppard started out doing small gigs at pubs and schools, and in November of 1978, they recorded a three-track EP. It was the EP that attracted Allen, and once they had a full lineup, Def Leppard cut their first album, a six-song offering called *Getcha Rocks Off*. The album was released in January of 1979 to an enthusiastic radio public. The band was immediately hailed as an up-and-coming power in the new wave of heavy metal. Later that same year, Def Leppard signed with the Vertigo label and completed their next album, *On Through the Night*, in just eighteen days. The album charted at number fifteen in the UK and number fifty-one in the U.S. and inspired the group to look toward the rich market across the Atlantic.

"Hello America," the hit single released in March of 1980, revealed Def Leppard's stateside intentions. The trend did not please the group's British fans, and the crowd threw bottles onto the stage in protest at an August concert. Undaunted, Def Leppard went on to a successful performance at the "Reading Rock 80" concert, with fellow hard rockers Gillian, Iron Maiden, Whitesnake, Krokus, Ozzy Osbourne, UFO, and Magnum.

Next on the docket was the September 1980 U.S. tour, opening for Ted Nugent, and Def Leppard began to win American fans wherever they played. When they returned from the U.S., the band hired a new producer, Robert "Mutt" Lange, and began recording *High 'N' Dry*. Lange and Def Leppard wanted the new album to be something of U.S. FM radio quality, and after three months of strenuous technical work, *High 'N' Dry* fit the bill. It broke into the American top forty and was followed up by a blockbuster tour with Blackfoot.

The success did not come without a cost, however. The relentless recording and touring took its toll on the group's unity and morale, and by the end of 1981, internal strife plagued Def Leppard. Willis was forced out the band halfway through the recording of the next album. The band replaced Willis with Phil Collen and completed *Pyromania* for its February 1982 release. The hit album sat at number two on the U.S. charts for weeks, edged out only by *Thriller*. *Pyromania* hit number eighteen in Britain, and Def Leppard embarked on a world tour and two years of fame and fortune.

Def Leppard stepped off their winning streak on New Year's Eve, 1984, just weeks after they had swept the American Music Awards. On December 31, drummer Rick Allen was involved in a serious car accident that ripped off his left arm. In the middle of recording, the band was devastated, but loyalty won out and Def Leppard refused to replace their faithful drummer. They decided to wait until Allen recovered to continue recording, though they were unsure if the one-armed drummer would even be able to play again.

In a little over a year and a half, and with the help of a specially designed drum set, Allen was back and so was Def Leppard, headlining at various rock festivals to adoring audiences. The band reentered the recording studio, and in August of 1987, the long awaited *Hysteria* made its way to the record stores. The British public had been waiting, and the album debuted at the pinnacle of their charts. The magic took longer, a lot longer, in the U.S., but forty-nine weeks after its release, *Hysteria* reached number one in the United States. (Only Fleetwood Mac's and Whitney Houston's eponymous albums have taken longer to reach the top.) The album also produced several hit singles, including the number two "Pour Some Sugar On Me," and a smash world tour. The schedule took its toll once again, however, and this time it was deadly.

The culprit once again was tension and strain, and the weapon alcohol. As Def Leppard entered the nineties, guitarist Steve Clark found himself increasingly dependent on alcohol to get him through. The hard, fast music was paralleled by a hard, fast lifestyle, and on January 8, 1991, the pace caught up with him. After a night of drinking with a friend Steve returned to his Chelsea flat to go to sleep. He never woke up. Found hours later by his girlfriend, Clark was pronounced dead due to alcohol-related respiratory failure.

Def Leppard waned as the nineties waxed.

Like many other heavy metal bands, they continued to record and maintain their core of metal fans, but they faded from the spotlight.

Clyde McPhatter

The Drifters were one of the trailblazers in the world of soul, combining a gospel style and a secular content to create an emotional, accessible style of music. Soul often merged with the rhythm and blues movement, and the Drifters enjoyed considerable success on the R&B charts. The Drifters took their name from the fact that all of the members of the band had drifted from group to group before coming together. One might have thought that once Clyde was on the boardwalk, it should have been an easy stroll to success. But the bottle stymied the singer, and he ended up falling off the street to stardom.

Clyde McPhatter was born on November 15, 1933, in Durham, North Carolina, into a musical and religious family. He started singing in church, developing his rich voice in the choir. Deciding to make music his life's work, Clyde set out in search of a group and eventually landed as a vocalist with the Dominoes. As the 1950's opened, McPhatter moved away from the Dominoes and began to

search for a new group—he found what he was looking for in a new ensemble called the Drifters. Here was an opportunity to return to his origins, to the gospel sounds of his childhood, while exploring the capabilities of the rhythm and blues sound.

Once assembled, the Drifters began recording almost immediately, and all six records that came out of the original Drifters reached the top ten on the R&B charts. "Money Honey" in 1953, "Such a Night," "Honey Love," and "White Christmas" in 1954, and "Whatcha Gonna Do" and a reprise of "White Christmas" in 1955 would all go down in the canon of rhythm and blues. Clyde was a driving force in the Drifters, contributing not only his sex-laden voice but also his impressive musical instincts and ideas. When Clyde was drafted into the army in 1954, the Drifters began to dissipate as a group. Without the glue that McPhatter provided, the group floundered and went through several lead singers in an attempt to replace Clyde. They failed to find a worthy heir to Clyde's voice and presence, and although the Drifters continued to record, they could not get anywhere near the charts. The Drifters disbanded in 1958.

The spirit of the Drifters did not die, and in 1959 a new version of the group emerged, with Ben E. King as the lead singer. This incarnation of the Drifters was even more successful than the first. In 1959, their single, "There Goes My Baby," hit number two, and in 1960 they topped the charts with "Save the Last Dance for Me." The group charted several more hits in the next few years and ended the string of triumphs with the number one smash single "Under the Boardwalk." This proved to be their last hit, but the song itself made several forays into the charts, covered by various artists for years to come.

Clyde McPhatter, meanwhile, had struck out on his own, pursuing a mildly successful solo career. His voice was heard crooning various R&B covers and originals, but he failed to recapture the glory he had experienced with the Drifters. He found that as the sixties progressed, the listening public turned away from the silky melodies of soul to the extravagance of the psychedelics and the political modernity of the hippies. The trend depressed Clyde, and he began to seek solace in the liquor bottle. Toward the end of the decade, the alcohol was interfering with the quality of McPhatter's ever smaller performances. At his worst, Clyde simply missed gigs. When he did show up, he often could not get through an entire set. His last attempts at recording were dismal failures.

In the end, alcohol killed Clyde McPhatter. The years of drinking took their toll on his heart, his kidneys, and his liver. He died on June 13, 1972, in the Bronx as a virtual unknown. Although the man had faded from the public eye, however, his influence on the music world can be seen even today, in the again popular sound of soul music.

Jim Morrison

The Lizard King answered to no one, and his antics won him an equal number of fans and foes. Beneath the sensationalism, however, Jim Morrison was taking countless artistic risks and using his talent and insight to break through to the other side. Eventually, his hard living sent him to the other side permanently, but his contributions to rock 'n' roll will be with us for eternity.

James Douglas Morrison was born on December 8, 1943, in Melbourne, Florida. Jim's father, a rear admiral in the U.S. Navy, moved the family throughout the country as he was transferred from base to base. In 1966, Jim graduated from Alexandria, Virginia's George Washington High School, restless and rebellious. He entered St. Petersburg Junior College and then transferred to Florida State University. The following year he dropped out and moved to Los Angeles, where he studied theater arts at UCLA. Poetry and philosophy interested him, particularly William Blake and Friedrich Nietzsche.

In 1964, while studying at UCLA, Jim met Ray Manzarek, a keyboard player who had been classically trained from the age of ten. Raised in Chicago, Ray had developed musical tastes in the direction of boogie-woogie and had spent much of his time in Chicago's south side blues clubs. He attended DePaul University, then transferred to UCLA when his family moved west. Ray and his brothers soon joined a blues band called Rick and the Ravens, and it was after a gig that Ray was approached by Jim Morrison.

Jim liked Ray's playing and Ray liked Jim's poetry, and the two spoke often of how such lyrics had never before been incorporated into a rock song. They formed a band in order to explore uncharted territory in the realm of rock lyrics, and they called themselves the Doors. The name was derived from Blake's line, "There are things that are known and things that are unknown; in between the doors," and from the book *The Doors of Perception*, Aldous Huxley's piece about mescaline experiments. Former Psychedelic Rangers drummer John Densmore, who Ray had met through his involvement with a transcendental meditation group, was soon added to the group.

In September 1965, the Doors recorded a demo of Morrison songs, "Moonlight Drive," "Summer's Almost Gone," "Break On Through," and "End of the Night" at World Pacific studios. Ray's two brothers and a female bass player had joined the group on the recording but left immediately afterwards because they disliked the material. Based on the demo, Columbia Records signed the Doors, and soon after guitarist Robby Krieger was invited to join the band and the lineup was complete. The quartet spent the next several months practicing and unsuccessfully looking for work, but the drought ended with a gig at the London Fog club on Sunset Boulevard. This led to a four month stint as the house band at the Whisky a Go-Go, during which time they obtained a release from Columbia and signed with Elektra. Soon after, the band was fired from the Whisky for performing Morrison's explicitly Oedipal "The End."

January 1967 saw the release of the Doors' eponymous debut album. Marked by Jim's psychosexual persona and a powerful rock/blues style, the band became an instant success through heavy FM radio play. The album rose to number two during a 121-week run on the charts. In July, "Light My Fire," (written by Krieger) was trimmed from its original length of almost seven minutes and released as a single. It topped the charts for three weeks, giving Elektra its first number one record.

Jim's aversion to authority was a commercial dilemma. While his drugged "Lizard King" persona frequently got him into trouble that included arrests for public obscenity and disorderly conduct, the younger generation loved him. In September 1967, while backstage in preparation for an appearance on *The Ed Sullivan Show*, the band was asked to change the line "girl, we couldn't get much higher" from "Light My Fire." They agreed, but Jim sang it anyway. Needless to say, the crowd roared.

Over the next few years, the Doors remained active, with a string of hit singles from the top ten albums, *Strange Days*, *Waiting for the Sun*, and *The Soft Parade*. By 1969, Jim's drinking and drug use had escalated to the point where it was impossible to predict what he would do on stage. Once he tumbled into the audience; another time he stopped singing and began to tell a series of humorless jokes. These incidents culminated in the April 1969 night in Miami when he allegedly exposed himself on stage. Jim was arrested by the FBI in Los Angeles and charged with interstate flight to avoid prosecution. Although the police had as evidence over 150 photographs, none showed exposure and the charges were eventually dropped. The damage had already been done, however, and the band lost nearly a million dollars in canceled tour dates.

In April 1970, the album *Morrison Hotel* hit U.S. number four and UK number twelve. One of the album's singles, "Queen of the Highway," was dedicated to Jim's new wife Pamela. Jim still found it necessary to create chaos, but his mischief became tiresome to the other members of the band. Substance abuse began to take a physical toll, and a weakened Morrison moved with his wife to Paris in March of 1971, three months before the release of the album, *L.A. Woman*. He called it retirement, saying that he wanted to write poetry in obscurity—though true obscurity was impossible since Simon and Schuster had already published two of his books: *An American Prayer* and *The Lords and the New Creatures*. The Doors continued to work and rehearse, anticipating Morrison's return. On July 3, 1971, however, Jim Morrison suffered a fatal alcohol-related heart attack in the bathtub of his third floor apartment, rue Beautreillis 17, near la Place de la Bastille.

Rumors abounded as many doubted that Morrison was actually dead. An anonymous doctor and no official autopsy, a sealed coffin, and an illegible death certificate made for dubious evidence in the minds of many fans. One of Jim's heroes was French poet Arthur Rimbaud, who gave up writing at age nineteen and wandered the world incognito. Many fans were positive that Jim had done the same.

Jim was buried in the poets' corner of the famous Père-Lachaise cemetery in Paris. His humble gravestone underwent a regular scrubbing to remove graffiti. In the eighties, his headstone was stolen, and a twenty-four-hour guard was installed to protect the sacred spot. The grave site attracts thousands of visitors annually, leaving in their wake a litter of trash, flowers, and love letters. This incursion prompted the cemetery, the final resting place also of such notables as Edith Piaf, Oscar Wilde, and Honoré de Balzac, to file a successful lawsuit to have Morrison's remains removed by the year 2001.

The surviving Doors released two albums, *Other Voices* and *Full Circle*, but it was painfully obvious that the band's soul had died with Jim, and in 1973 the Doors broke up for good. On April 25, 1974, Pamela Courson Morrison died in Hollywood of a heroin overdose. Jim's cult following remains strong, generating numerous books, steady record sales, induction into the Rock 'n' roll Hall of Fame, and a major motion picture by Oliver Stone in 1991. The Doors continue to make the charts with new releases like *Greatest Hits*, *Alive*, *She Cried*, and a complete box set. If he is alive today, Jim Morrison is surely impressed by his own legacy.

Gene Vincent

Gene Vincent, bebop artist extraordinaire, traveled a rough road in his quest for stardom. He was responsible for several household hits, but he never seemed to reap the rewards of his contributions.

On February 11, 1935, Vincent Eugene Craddock was born in Norfolk, Virginia, where he sang in church, listened to country music, and learned to play the guitar. When Gene was sixteen, he quit school and lied about his age so he could join the U.S. Navy and fight in the Korean War. Stationed at Norfolk Naval Base, Gene was serving as a dispatch rider when he had a serious motorcycle accident and almost lost his left leg. The doctors wanted to amputate, but Gene refused and his leg was saved. He was forced to wear a cast for months, then a metal leg brace, and he walked with a painful limp for the rest of his life. After he was released from the Navy in May 1955, he spent several months in the hospital, where he devoted his convalescence to his renewed interest in music. Once out of the hospital, Gene decided to pursue a singing career and he started to hang around radio station WCMS in an attempt to establish himself in the Norfolk country scene.

His initial exposure came from occasional guest appearances with the house band and developed into regular broadcasts that helped perfect

Gene's rockabilly style. In 1956, he met "Sheriff" Tex Davis, a DJ from WCMS who helped Gene record his first demo. The demo included "Be-Bop-A-Lula," "Race with the Devil," and "I Sure Miss You." In April 1956, the demo won Capitol Record's Elvis Sound-Alike Sweepstakes, securing a record contract for Vincent. The Blue Caps, the musicians who backed Gene on the demo, agreed to join him in his future musical endeavors, and the group headed to a Nashville studio to begin recording.

In June, Gene Vincent and the Blue Caps made their record debut with "Woman Love" on the A side and "Be-Bop-A-Lula" on side B. It was the B side that caught on, and "Be-Bop-A-Lula" raced up the charts to number seven. Several weeks later the band played their first show, beginning a hectic year of nonstop touring, several singles and an album, and a film debut with *The Girl Can't Help It.* In the midst of all this success, Gene Vincent and the Blue Caps soon became recognized as one of the wildest rock bands in the business, on stage and off. Gene's pace began to catch up with him, but though the doctors advised him to slow down when his leg started acting up, Gene ignored their advice. In January 1957, the pain grew too great and Gene was hospitalized for three weeks.

Even after Gene was released from the hospital, he could not return to work for several months. The band got a much needed vacation, but the break had not come soon enough for guitarist Cliff Gallup, who had quit the band when he could no longer take the intense pressure and exhausting schedule. Sure enough, when Gene got back on his feet, he reverted almost immediately to the old fast-paced routine. The Blue Caps developed a reputation for violence—they destroyed dressing rooms, set fires backstage, and incited riots at many of their shows. Flagrant mismanagement and a never-ending procession of temporary musicians plagued the band as well.

When "Lotta Lovin'" hit number thirteen on the charts in September of 1957, it seemed that the band might make a comeback. The success, however, was short-lived. Gene's personal problems, compounded by persistent drinking, made him moody and unpredictable until November 1958, when the band finally broke up.

Determined to continue his musical career, Gene revamped his image, adopting a black leather look, and entered the studio as a solo artist. In December 1959, Vincent moved to England and found that the British audiences were just as welcoming and enthusiastic as they had been in the early days. Gene's path was not fated to be easy, though, and as soon as he completed a successful European tour, he was involved in a tragic automobile accident. He and friend Eddie Cochran were returning to London after a late show on April 17, 1960. Eddie was killed and Gene sustained critical injuries.

Gene's alcohol dependence was exacerbated by the torment that resulted from his friend's death, and the quality of his performances became erratic. Although he recorded several more UK hits like "Pistol Packin' Mama" and "She She Little Sheila," his stage appearances were infrequent and traumatic. He clearly favored his leg, and his bloodcurdling screams were provoked by true agony.

By the end of the 1960's, Gene's life had completely fallen apart. Deep in debt, involved in a new management dispute, and facing an oversaturated audience, he disappeared from sight. Several previously recorded tracks were released during the artist's hibernation, but none were successful enough to induce a resurfacing. In the fall of 1971, Gene's fourth wife left him and his health began to fail, both results of his alcoholism. He entered the Inter-Valley Community Hospital in New Hahall, California for bleeding ulcers. Soon after he entered the hospital, the ulcers began to hemorrhage. Gene Vincent's life came to an end on October 12, 1971.

At the time of his death, "Be-Bop-A-Lula" had sold over nine million copies, but because of various legal disputes, Vincent died broke and disillusioned. In 1980, the last four songs that Gene had recorded were released, as well as a box set and several other retrospective offerings.

Chapter 3

.

Heart Stoppers

Bobby Darin

Bobby Darin will never be considered a rock 'n' roll legend. However, he overcame poverty and rheumatic fever to carve out a multidimensional career in which he eventually distinguished himself as a talented singer, songwriter, and Academy Award nominee. Bobby was one to attack life with enormous courage and heart. Ironically, it was his heart that cut short his inspirational life story.

Bobby Darin was born Walden Robert Cassotto on May 14, 1936, in a tough area of the Bronx. Raised by his mother, a onetime professional dancer, Bobby's education included exposure to the piano, drums, bass, guitar, and vibes. He was also an excellent student, winning a scholarship to study science and drama at Hunter College. During college, Bobby began singing and playing the piano in New York supper clubs. With the taste of show business fresh in his mouth, Bobby let his college career fall by the wayside.

In 1956, music producer Don Kirshner set up an audition with Connie Francis' manager George Scheck, who gave Darin a contract with Decca Records. This association was not a fruitful one, producing four flop singles. In 1957, with Kirshner's help, Darin signed with Atco Records, but his first three Atco singles were also relative failures.

In 1958, Bobby Darin was afraid that Atco was going to drop him, and endeavoring to protect himself, he wrote and recorded the song "Early in the Morning" with a group called the Ding Dongs. He sold the recording to Brunswick Records, but it turned out that hedging his bets would not be necessary. Soon after he made the deal with Brunswick, Bobby's newest Atco release, "Splish Splash," shot through the roof on the American and British charts. "Early in the Morning" was released under the Atco name and moved slowly up the charts. The success of "Splish Splash" spawned an avalanche of follow-up hits which included "Queen of the Hop," "Dream Lover," "Beyond the Sea," and "Mack the Knife," which topped the charts on both sides of the Atlantic. In 1959, Darin won two Grammy Awards: Best New Male Artist and Best Vocal Performance, Male.

In 1960, Bobby married actress Sandra Dee. By this time, Darin was one of the most highly paid nightclub performers in America and also very active in movies and television. His film credits include *Too Late Blues, Come September, Hell Is for Heroes*, and *Captain Newman, M.D.*, for which he received an Oscar nomination.

Although Darin was comfortable with both adult and teenage audiences, he took dead aim at the latter in the late '60's with a string of folk-rock songs including "If I Were a Carpenter." This foray into what was at the time a lucrative musical direction was lambasted by many, including Tim Hardin, who considered Darin an opportunist.

Bobby divorced Sandra Dee in the late '60's and turned his attention to politics, working extensively for Robert Kennedy during the 1968 presidential campaign. Shaken by Kennedy's assassination, he claimed he had a mystical experience at the funeral which prompted him to sell all his possessions and retreat to a caravan at Big Sur. After a year of contemplation, Darin rejoined society and started his own label, Direction Records.

Bobby Darin had a history of heart problems dating back to his boyhood rheumatic fever. On December 12, 1973, he was admitted to Cedars of Lebanon Hospital in Los Angeles for an examination. Tests showed that an artificial valve that had been inserted two years earlier was not functioning properly. On December 29, 1973, at 12:15 A.M., after almost seven hours on the operating table, Bobby Darin died of heart complications.

Bobby Darin's star on the Hollywood Walk of Fame is located at 1735 Vine Street. His body was donated to science.

Cass Elliot

By combining flowing harmonies with thoughtful lyrics, the Mamas and the Papas were able to create a sound that will surely withstand the test of time. But although they brought the sound of folk into the mainstream without compromising the integrity of the genre, they did sacrifice the main Mama, Cass Elliot.

Born on September 19, 1941, in Baltimore, Maryland, Ellen Naomi Cass eventually found international fame as "Mama Cass Elliot." Because of her father's food-service business (serving construction workers), Cass' family moved around a lot when she was growing up. Smart as well as talented, Cass started taking piano lessons but switched to guitar when she discovered folk music. Everything seemed to come easily to Cass, and whether it was a part in a summer stock theater, her first singing job (within a few weeks of her arrival in New York), or a spot in a road production of *The Music Man*, she was at ease in the world of entertainment. As a student at American University in Washington, D.C., Cass married

James (not Jimi) Hendricks to get him out of the draft.

In 1963, the couple formed a band called the Big Three and released two unsuccessful records for the FM label. The group evolved into the Mugwumps, as Denny Doherty joined their musical project. When the album they recorded for Warner Brothers was not released, the group split up; two of the members started the Lovin' Spoonful, and Cass spent a short time in a jazz trio. In January 1965, Denny joined John and Michelle Phillips in the New Journeymen, and the three of them spent a short time in the Virgin Islands. They lived in tents on the beach while they revised and rehearsed the group, concentrating on their vocal sound and harmony. Cass showed up a few weeks later but she refused to go on stage with them. Instead, she got a job waitressing where they performed, and she sang her parts from the tables.

When the money ran out, the group moved out to Los Angeles and stayed with their friend Barry McGuire. Cass finally agreed to join the group, and Barry offered his financial help after hearing them perform. He introduced them to his producer, Lou Adler, the owner of Dunhill Records. Adler was so impressed with their audition that he offered them a contract the very next day. Inspired by their unique two male/two female lineup and by the Hell's Angels who called their women "mamas," the group changed their name to the Mamas and the Papas. Within a few months, they were recording their first album, *If You Can Believe Your Eyes and Ears*.

Friends like the Byrds and the Lovin' Spoonful were topping the charts, and the Mamas and the Papas knew that their turn would come. It was December 1965 when the Mamas and the Papas entered the charts with *California Dreamin'*, which featured catchy pop tunes and intricate harmonies. By March it was a million-selling, blockbuster hit. They released a single in May, "Monday, Monday," which reached number one on the charts. Over the next three years, the group turned out forty top-forty singles and four top-ten albums. Some of these hits remain classics like "Words of Love," "Dedicated to the One I Love," and "I Saw Her Again Last Night." Many of them were autobiographical, including "Creeque Alley," which tells the story of the creation and history of the group.

In 1967, Cass took time off to have her baby, Owen Vanessa, on April 26, but she was back by June when the Mamas and the Papas became a major factor in organizing the Monterey Pop Fes-

tival. Later that year, the group canceled their UK appearance after Cass was arrested upon their arrival in England. She spent the night in jail, but the charges, stealing two keys and two blankets worth less than $20, were dropped the next day. It was a sign of the trouble to come, however, and although the popularity continued, John and Michelle's failing marriage, the desire for new creative outlets, and various other personal conflicts were tearing the group apart. Following the release of the number twelve hit, "Dream a Little Dream," near the end of 1968, the Mamas and the Papas broke up.

Following the split, Cass, who had been overweight since childhood, lost 110 pounds in less than a year. She was preparing for her solo debut in Las Vegas. The extreme weight loss, however, made her seriously ill and the show was canceled. In 1969, Cass had two top-forty hits with "It's Getting Better" and "Make Your Own Kind of Music." She followed them up with three albums on the Dunhill label, a duet album with Dave Mason in 1971, and a switch to a new label—RCA. Her continued success came more from TV appearances and nightclub performances than from her mediocre record sales. When she received a standing ovation at the end of a sold-out, two-week engagement at the London Palladium, it seemed that Cass had triumphed over her various setbacks. That was not, unfortunately, the truth.

Just two days after the London show, on July 29, 1974, Cass Elliot was found dead in Harry Nilsson's flat, where she had been staying. Although popular opinion holds that Elliot choked on a ham sandwich, the truth is that she succumbed to a heart attack. Mama Cass was ultimately a victim of her lifestyle and, with her death, the music industry lost a guiding light.

Lowell George

Little Feat has always been above all else a concert band. Their sound synthesizes a variety of influences, including country-western, Dixieland, R&B, and classic rock. The band has enjoyed a gradual evolution and remarkable longevity; after several years apart they reunited in 1988 and returned to doing what they do best—performing in front of a crowd. Unfortunately, they were missing Lowell George, who had not realized that when you're a fat man in a bathtub, it's easy to slip.

Lowell George, born in 1939 in Hollywood, California, was a cofounder of Little Feat, along with Roy Estrada. Lowell graduated from Hollywood High School and became a session musician. Lowell ran into Roy Estrada when the two were playing in Frank Zappa's Mothers of Invention. When the Mothers broke up, the two decided to strike out on their own. They gathered a solid group of musicians and created a band under the name of "Country Zeke and the Freaks." Lowell George was the lead vocalist and guitarist, and Roy Estrada played the bass. They were joined by Richard Hayward on the drums and Bill Payne on the keyboard.

The band had their first gig in the LA psychedelic club known as Temple of the Rainbow. Soon they found that, because of their name, they were being mis-billed as a country band, so the search began for a new handle. George and Estrada decided on Little Feat after recalling the time that Jimmy Carl Black, drummer for the Mothers, had teased Lowell about his "little feet." They changed an "e" to an "a" and "Country Zeke and the Freaks" streamlined into "Little Feat."

Lowell George as the primary songwriter and lead vocalist soon emerged as the group's leader. Several of his original songs were featured on their eponymous debut album, released in November of 1970 under the Warner/Reprise label. "Willin' " and "Forty-four Blues/How Many Years" were two of the highlights of the album. The latter presented an impressive dual guitar piece, with Ry Cooder joining George for the session. The debut album met a favorable response, and the success was augmented by the accompanying tour, when the group began to make a name for itself as a concert band. Lowell George songs were hitting the charts with the help of other artists as well—in 1970, the Byrds recorded his "Little Truck Stop Girl" on their album *Untitled*.

Little Feat had begun the climb to the top in 1970, but it was 1972 before they had attracted worldwide attention. Their 1972 offering, *Sailin' Shoes*, emphasized the blues elements of the Little Feat sound. In the process, the album won the high praise of one of the princes of rock 'n' roll, Mick Jagger, who named Little Feat among his favorite bands. Many of his countrymen followed suit, and Little Feat always enjoyed wider success in Britain than in the U.S. The bulk of *Sailin' Shoes* came from George's pen; some of the most notable George originals included "Cold, Cold, Cold," "Sailin' Shoes," "Easy to Slip," and "Tripe Face Boogy."

Nineteen seventy-two was a year not only of unprecedented success but also of integral lineup changes. Estrada left the group and three new members came aboard: Kenny Gradney replaced Estrada on the bass and Sam Clayton offered his talents to the rhythm section, playing the conga and various other percussion instruments. Paul Barrere joined as a supplementary vocalist and guitarist to allow Lowell George to turn the majority of his attention to songwriting. George contributed significantly to the 1973 album *Dixie Chicken*, offering the title song and "Fat Man in the Bathtub." Soon, however, he began to write songs primarily for other artists. *Dixie Chicken* heralded a move toward the Dixieland and jazz sounds, created in part by the "Tower of Power" horn section.

Little Feat had their sailin' shoes on; they produced successful albums and even more successful tours. The 1974 release, *Feats Don't Fail Me Now*, featured increased songwriting contributions from Bill Payne and Paul Barrere. The former offered the title track and "Oh Atlanta," and the latter penned "Skin It Back." As other members of the group began to come into their own, George retreated into the background. The process was not a hostile one, it was rather that George felt confident in the talents of his band mates and consequently felt comfortable passing over the reins. The extra time gave him a chance to explore other areas of performance.

The Last Record Album, released in 1975, embodied the graceful transition. The album featured two Lowell tunes, "Down Below the Border Line" and "Long Distance Love." The rest of the tracks were the creations of Payne and Barrere. The album sold well, but its success did not adequately reflect the glory of the sellout tour. The next album told the same story—the performance on the charts did not match the live success. *Time Loves a Hero* was released in 1977 and was a compilation primarily of Barrere's work, and the album fared better overseas than in the United States.

The disparity between recorded and live success was bridged in part with the release of a live LP, *Waiting for Columbus*, in 1978. The record came close to capturing the magical strength of Little Feat's live performances. Success on the charts finally came, and *Waiting for Columbus* was declared a gold record. The public indisputably recognized Little Feat for their innovative contributions to the rock world. In 1979, Bill Payne said, "People would always say to us, 'This album sounds different from the last one,' and they *were* different." Little Feat had made a name for themselves through their constant reinventions, and Lowell George had been the one to set this precedent of continual evolution.

While Lowell George scaled back his songwriting for Little Feat, he did not curb his creative impulses entirely. Nor did he curb his habit of overeating. He began working on a solo album entitled, appropriately, *Thanks I'll Eat It Here* while in the midst of recording the next Little Feat release. This double duty would eventually prove too much for the songster to handle. In his many years of service to and performance with Little Feat, Lowell George had run his body into the ground. In 1979, he weighed an unmanageable 300 pounds, was recovering from hepatitis, and was taking any number of prescription drugs. On June 29, 1979, the combination of stresses on the body of Lowell George proved to be too much. The official cause of death was a heart attack after a strenuous performance that night in Washington, D.C. Those in the know seem to think, however, that drugs may have been involved and that various prescription drugs were found in George's hotel room when the body was found. The bottles had been removed by the time the police arrived.

Regardless, Lowell George can be credited with years of intense contributions to the music industry. Appropriately, the contributions did not cease with Lowell's death. He had completed his solo work and recorded enough of his vocals for the Little Feat album for both records to be released on schedule. And in 1981, a retrospective album included some George originals that had been previously unreleased. Most notable among these finds was "Sweet China White," a bluesy song which now stands among the numerous Lowell George creations as a testament to his tireless work and his boundless creativity.

Andy Gibb

As the brother of the Bee Gees, Andy Gibb understood that music is thicker than water. His love songs took him to the top, and he added a country-western slant to the disco dance sound to carve out a unique place for himself in the world of rock 'n' roll. Sadly, Gibb never had a chance to enjoy this place, as the fast lane of rock 'n' roll made it tough for him to stay alive.

When Andrew Roy Gibb was born into the Gibb family on March 5, 1958, in Manchester, England, he was instantly initiated into the world of music. He was just six months old when the family moved to Brisbane, Australia, where his life was dominated by the artistic atmosphere established by his father, a big-band leader; his mother, a singer; and his three older brothers, Robin, Maurice, and Barry. When Andy was five, his brothers hit the Australian music scene, calling themselves the Bee Gees. Within a short time, the family returned to England to accommodate the brothers' growing fame.

It was difficult for Andy to adjust to his new life, as his classmates resented the fame of his brothers. This is not surprising, considering that a chauffeur-driven Rolls Royce dropped him off in front of the school each day. Andy was thirteen when his family moved again, this time to Spain. It was in this new country that Andy's brothers gave him his first guitar and taught him how to play. When he finally performed in front of an audience, singing cover tunes at a local bar, he quickly decided that he had found his life's work. After only a few more years, Andy dropped out of school in order to concentrate on his music full-time.

In 1973, Andy played with the Bee Gees, but the band did not offer him the niche that he desired. His brothers encouraged him to try a solo act, and with their help and support, it did not take Andy long to follow their successful lead. Andy's first record was *Words and Music*, released on the ATA label in 1975. He followed this up with a tour with the Bay City Rollers and then did a stint as the opening act for Sweet. His brothers continued to support him and by 1976 he had a demo tape of his own originals. Less than a year later, Andy secured a recording contract with RSO Records, which also handled the Bee Gees.

Andy was only nineteen years old when he made his RSO album debut with *Flowing Rivers*, produced by his brother Barry. The music combined a flavor of the disco craze with a bit of the country-rock influence (the Eagles were recording at the same studio at the same time). The sound caught on, and Andy made it to the top of the charts in July 1977 with his first single, "I Want to Be Your Everything," which was written by Barry. The follow-up was another triumph; Andy's "(Love) Is Thicker Than Water" replaced the Bee Gees' "Stayin' Alive" in the number one spot in March of 1978.

Over the next few months, Andy's career skyrocketed. His next album spent time in the top ten, and his third single, "Shadow Dancing," reached the top of the charts in June. With that success, Andy became the only artist to date whose first three singles had all reached number one. Just a month later, the Bee Gees joined Andy on stage in Miami. It was the first time that all four brothers had appeared together in public.

Good-looking and clean-cut, Andy was the perfect teen idol. He maintained his recording success, releasing two platinum albums and two top-ten singles. "An Everlasting Love" hit number five, and "(Our Love) Don't Throw It All Away" reached number nine. In 1980 there were several more hits, including "Desire" at number four and

"I Can't Help It" with Olivia Newton-John reaching number twelve. His next album, *Andy Gibb's Greatest Hits*, went gold in record time, and Andy seemed unstoppable.

As the eighties progressed, however, Andy's life began to fall apart. RSO was in financial trouble, and Andy's cocaine habit was adversely affecting the quality of his work. Andy turned out two more successful singles: "Time is Time" and "Me (Without You)" were his last two top-forty hits. Aware of his slipping career, Andy moved to Los Angeles to be with girlfriend Victoria Principal and to explore different aspects of the entertainment business. He made his stage debut in *The Pirates of Penzance* on June 10, 1981. He kept his finger in the music industry and recorded a mildly successful duet with Victoria in the fall.

Next Andy made a brief foray into the world of television, replacing Dionne Warwick as the cohost of *Solid Gold*. By this time, however, Andy's life was spinning out of control and soon he was fired from *Solid Gold* for missing too many shows. Andy fell into a deep depression, and when Victoria left him in 1985, Andy checked into the Betty Ford Clinic. Andy won his battle against his cocaine addiction, but he left the clinic clean and broke. A year after he left rehab, Andy filed bankruptcy papers in Miami, claiming to have over $1 million in debts and less than $50,000 in assets.

Always a fighter, Andy refused to give up, in spite of overwhelming odds. In 1988, he signed a contract with Island Records and went back to work. Before he could carry out his brave comeback plans, however, he began to experience severe stomach pains. On March 7, 1988, he was rushed to John Radcliffe Hospital in Oxford and diagnosed with a cardiac infection. Three days later, at the age of thirty, Andy Gibb died in his hospital bed.

Bill Haley

Bill Haley, one of the founding fathers of rock, challenged the world of music with a combination of country, western, and rhythm and blues that produced the first rock 'n' roll hit.

It all started on July 6, 1925, when William John Clifton Haley was born in Highland Park, Michigan. Bill's early musical education was comprised of the country songs his parents loved. His mother gave piano lessons and accompanied his father on banjo or mandolin. When he was seven, Bill's parents gave him his first guitar. During the Great Depression, Bill's father lost his job, but he found work in Boothwyn, Pennsylvania. Resuming his musical progress in his new home, Bill taught himself to yodel, resulting in a solo act by the time he was thirteen.

He started out as "The Rambling Yodeller," performing at talent contests, dances, and fairs. Soon thereafter, he joined his first band and began playing guitar for a local radio personality, Cousin Lee. Bill's big break arrived when he answered a "Musician Wanted" ad in *Billboard* magazine and got a job in a prominent Midwest band called the Downhomers. His next four years were busy ones, as he toured all over the country with several different C&W bands and a traveling medicine show.

In 1946, at the age of twenty-one, Bill quit the band, married Dorothy Crow, and moved back home to Pennsylvania. Within a year, Bill was working as a DJ on WPWA and he had a new band called the Four Aces of the Western Swing to accompany him on his radio show. Finally, in 1948, he made his recording debut with "Too Many Parties, Too Many Pals" (by Hank Williams) on Cowboy Records. He followed that up with two more singles before the band broke up.

In the next few years, Bill Haley began to explore dance hall blues, combining it with his country sound, and the result was the earliest incarnation of rock 'n' roll. The new sound showed itself again and again as Haley rehearsed and performed with His Comets. Nineteen fifty-one saw a rock 'n' roll version of Jackie Brenston's "Rocket 88." Haley was encouraged by the reactions that he got with the tune and continued down the trail of rock 'n' roll. In 1952 he released "Rock the Joint" and in 1953 "Crazy, Man, Crazy." Both tapped into the seething teen culture waiting for an idol, and for a while it seemed that Bill Haley and His Comets would be just that.

"Rock Around the Clock" was Bill Haley's next offering, but the single failed to make the charts. Haley persevered and followed it up with "Shake, Rattle and Roll," which reached number seven. He decided to give "Rock Around the Clock" a chance to ride on the coattails of his latest hit and rereleased it. The gamble paid off and "Rock Around the Clock" shot up the charts. It has in fact made seven separate appearances on the Billboard charts—including stints as part of the *American Graffiti* soundtrack and as the *Happy Days* theme song.

Unfortunately, the clock was unkind to Bill Haley. When "Rock Around the Clock" came out in 1955, he was already an overweight thirty-year-old. He did chart two more hits—"Burn That Candle" and "See You Later, Alligator"—but his momentum was gone. Bill Haley and His Comets were eclipsed by the younger and sexier rockers of the day: Elvis, Little Richard, Chuck Berry.

Bill Haley continued to perform, mostly in oldies shows and on European tours. His records continued to sell—60 million by the time he died—and Haley and His Comets maintained a small but loyal core of fans.

As Bill Haley the musician faded from the limelight, so did Bill Haley the man fade from life. He had always been a heavy drinker, and his slow decline added paranoia and depression to his alcoholic tendencies. As he grew older, his behavior grew increasingly strange, and it has been said that he painted the windows of his home black and installed floodlights to deter intruders.

On February 9, 1981, Bill Haley's slow burning candle was finally extinguished. He died in his Texas home of a heart attack. On that day, the world of rock 'n' roll lost not one of its biggest stars, but one of its first.

O'Kelly Isley

Since the 1950's, generations of R&B lovers have been twisting and shouting to the Isley Brothers, with their tight sound and engaging stage performances. Even though they continue to perform and record today, their songs are often rerecorded into chart-busting hits by scores of other artists. The passing of O'Kelly Isley, Jr., one of the founding members of the group, has called for the Isley story to be told.

O'Kelly Isley, Sr., announced when he married his wife, Sally Bernice Bell, that he wanted to have sons who would sing their way into the shoes left by the Mills Brothers. The Mills Brothers were a pop group based in Cincinnati, and O'Kelly envisioned his own Cincinnati family continuing the tradition. Sure enough, the Isley boys were musically inclined, getting their start singing in gospel choirs and as a trio with their mother's piano accompaniment. O'Kelly Jr., Rudolph, and Ronald traveled around Ohio and Kentucky making their music until 1956 when they set off for the Big Apple.

Getting started in the big city music industry was more difficult than they imagined, and the three brothers took odd jobs to sustain themselves as they searched for their musical break. Their persistence paid off, and in the beginning of 1957 they were given a spot at the Apollo Theater in Harlem. The performance was followed up by a recording session with the Teenage label, with the single "Angels Cried" as the product. The Isley Brothers embarked on a tour of the East Coast, playing at various black theaters in the major cities. Producer George Goldner bought their contract, and they recorded several singles under his Mark X, Cindy, and Gone labels.

Although none of these songs took off, the Isleys came out of this era with the key to their future success. They realized that in order to attract attention, they had to capitalize on the energy and rhythms of the live performances of the R&B masters. "Shout" was inspired by a performance by Jackie Wilson at the Howard Theater in Washington, D.C. Ron Isley wrote the song as a testament to Wilson's ability to rally a crowd, and it became the group's first hit when it was released by RCA in the summer of 1959.

The magic of live performances soon became one of the Isley Brothers' claims to fame. They had boundless energy and enthusiasm and a charisma that attracted the admiration of, among others, James Brown. He wrote in his autobiography, "We saw the Isley Brothers coming from the back of the theater, swinging on ropes, like Tarzan, onto the stage. They hardly had to sing at all. They'd already killed 'em." The Isleys attracted the attention of other notables, and in 1963 the Beatles recorded their own version of the Isley Brothers' original, "Twist and Shout," after hearing it on the radio in the UK. The Beatles became fans and met the Isley Brothers when they came to England on a tour of the UK. In 1964, the Beatles' "Twist and Shout" hit number two on the British charts.

The mid-sixties were years of growth for the Isleys, now residents of Teaneck, New Jersey. They named their newly formed record label after their new home: T-Neck. In 1964, they were graced by the talents of Jimi Hendrix, who was a member of the band for a short time before his meteoric rise to fame. Soon after Jimi left, the Isley Brothers signed on to Berry Gordy's Motown Records label. Gordy, recognizing the potential of the Isleys, assigned them to his top songwriter producers—the team of Holland, Dozier, and Holland. The team gave the Isley Brothers their first Motown single, "This Old Heart of Mine (Is Weak for You)," as well as ten compositions for their first Motown album. Soon, however, the Isley Brothers were pulled from the top-ranked songwriting team after some of the other Motown artists expressed jealousy.

The Isleys proceeded to leave Motown and released their next single, "It's Your Thing," under their own T-Neck label. "It's Your Thing" proved to be their biggest hit and garnered them a Grammy in 1969 for "best rhythm and blues vocal by a duo or group." The song featured a new crop of Isleys, with younger brothers Ernie and Marvin and brother-in-law Chris Jasper joining the original trio. The success of "It's Your Thing" attracted other artists to the T-Neck label, and the Isley dynasty continued to grow. They played to a sold-out Yankee Stadium in the summer of 1969 in a performance that proved to be a high point in their career.

The addition of the younger Isleys coincided with a new musical direction, as the Isley Brothers began to experiment with a more pop-oriented sound. Their cover of the Stephen Stills hit, "Love the One You're With," made the top twenty and featured the acoustic sound of Ernie's guitar. The Isley Brothers lineup became known as the 3+3 structure, with the original trio supplemented and enhanced by the three newcomers. The younger members brought to the group their considerable musical training, expanding the range of influences to include jazz and classical music. A contemporary inspiration was Stevie Wonder's *Music of My Mind*. The idea of a concept album appealed to the Isleys, and they traveled to Los Angeles to record *3+3*. The album proved to be a raging success, and with its combination of original and cover material was one of the first albums by black artists to go platinum, selling over two million copies.

The Isleys continued to enjoy renown in R&B as well as in pop circles. They packed stadiums across the country, from Madison Square Garden in New York City to the Forum in Los Angeles. They hit the number four spot on the pop charts in 1975 with their spirited single "Fight the Power."

The honeymoon could not last forever, though, and in 1984 the two trios parted ways. The younger three stayed on to record on the CBS label as Isley/Jasper/Isley. The original trio signed with Warner Brothers, but before they could record anything, the grim reaper took his toll. In 1986, the Isley Brothers lost one of their founding members when O'Kelly Isley died of a heart attack. He went to sleep in his Teaneck, New Jersey, home and never woke up.

Roy Orbison

Unlike many popular singers of his day, Roy Orbison, "The Big O," was not a teen idol. Always appealing more to a mature audience, Orbison was nonetheless regarded as a member of the original "rockabilly royalty" and his music remains a strong influence on contemporary artists.

Born in Vernon, Texas, on April 23, 1936, Roy grew up with parents who encouraged his love of music. They gave him his first guitar on his sixth birthday, and his dad taught him some basic chords. Even as a child, Roy showed talent and commitment, and by the time he was eight he was making regular weekend appearances on KVWC Radio in Vernon. At age ten Roy performed before live audiences at local gigs and talent shows. When his family moved to Wink, Texas, Roy formed his first band, the Wink Westerners. In spite of his love of music, however, Roy did not intend to make it his career.

In 1954, Roy left for North Texas State, planning to become a teacher. It was there that he met Pat Boone, who encouraged his musical endeavors and steered him toward a rockabilly sound. The two friends formed a band called the Teen Kings, and after winning a "battle of the bands" competition in 1955, they made their television debut in Odessa. The broadcast by local stations across Texas gave the Teen Kings a great deal of exposure and enabled them to record their first single, "Ooby Dooby." Released on Je-Wel in Texas, the record did not sell well, but it did bring Roy to the attention of several well-known artists including Jerry Lee Lewis, Johnny Cash, and Elvis Presley. In 1956, Cash set Roy up for an audition with Sam Phillips of Sun Records in Memphis. This meeting led to a contract, and when "Ooby Dooby" was rereleased it reached number fifty-nine on the charts.

Hoping for another Elvis, Phillips released three more unsuccessful singles, pushing Roy to sing rockabilly even though it did not naturally suit his voice. After touring with Cash, Lewis, and Carl Perkins, Roy departed Sun and went to work as a staff songwriter at Acuff-Rose Music. One of his first efforts was "Claudette" (written for his wife), which was recorded by the Everly Brothers on the B side of "All I Have to Do Is Dream." The record reached number thirty and sold several million copies worldwide.

In 1959, Roy moved to Monument Records, where the next year his "Only the Lonely" sold over two million copies and charted at number two. This was followed by a string of top-ten singles: "Running Scared, "Cryin'," "Dream Baby," "In Dreams," "It's Over," and "Mean Woman Blues." His 1964 release, "Oh, Pretty Woman," sold over seven million copies and topped the charts on both sides of the Atlantic. During these years, Roy spent time touring with the Beatles, Elvis, and the Rolling Stones.

Showing an interest in both movies and television, Roy signed with MGM records, a label which could provide access to both. The affiliation, however, was anything but fruitful—the highlights were a mild hit, "Ride Away," and a silly 1961 film, *Fastest Guitar Alive*, in which he played a role meant originally for Elvis. The year 1966 was also the beginning of a series of tragedies that reshaped Roy's life. On June 6, as he and his wife raced their motorcycles through the countryside near Gallatin, Tennessee, the twenty-five-year-old Claudette was struck by a pickup truck and killed. Two years later, two of his three sons were playing with a lighter and a model airplane when a corner of their bedding ignited. The flames quickly spread, destroying their Hendersonville, Tennessee, home and killing Roy Jr. and Tony.

Roy was shattered by the tragic turn of events, and he reacted by throwing himself into his work. He began touring extensively and his life began to turn around. On a 1969 European tour, Roy met and married his second wife, Barbara. They had a son, Roy Kelton. Roy remained faithful to his own traditional musical style, in spite of the changes in his life, and in the musical taste of the public. Though still immensely popular in Europe, Roy rarely made the U.S. charts in the seventies. He seldom toured in the United States, and he refused to take part in any revival shows. He played country music when he played anything, and at the end of the decade, he stopped playing altogether for health reasons. He found himself on the operating table in 1979 for open-heart surgery, and it seemed that Orbison had seen the last of his musical career.

That, however, was not the case. After a speedy recovery, Roy Orbison and Emmylou Harris scored a hit country duet with "That Lovin' You Feeling Again." Later that year, Orbison opened for the Eagles in the West Coast portion of their tour. As the eighties progressed, Orbison continued his slow rise from the ashes and in 1987 he signed with Virgin and released a concert film with Elvis Costello, Bruce Springsteen, and Tom Waits. The year 1988 saw him join the Traveling Wilburys, along with Bob Dylan, Tom Petty, Jeff Lynne, and George Harrison. *Volume One* was the result of the collaboration, and the album stands as a lasting testament to Roy Orbison's musical development and maturity.

While with the Traveling Wilburys, Roy continued to record as a solo artist as well, and *Mystery Girl* was finished soon after *Volume One*. Roy would not live to see his solo album released. Roy Orbison had a heart attack and dropped dead on December 6, 1988. Two months later, *Mystery Girl* was released and one of its singles, "You Got It," hit number nine on the charts. It was Roy Orbison's first top-ten hit in twenty-three years.

Chapter 4

.

Murder, She Wrote

Sam Cooke

Sam Cooke's velvety voice and effortless style allowed him to make a smooth transition from gospel to the secular sound of soul. His sudden exit from this world was as mysterious as it was tragic, and we are left to imagine what a wonderful world rock 'n' roll might have been had a romantic rendezvous ended differently.

Sam Cooke was born on January 22, 1931, in Clarksdale, Mississippi. The son of a minister, Sam moved with his family to Chicago when his father accepted a job at the Church of Christ Holiness. At an early age Sam began singing in the church choir, and by his ninth birthday Sam joined the Singing Children with one of his four brothers and two of his three sisters. In high school, Sam and his brother joined a gospel group called the Highway QC's. The Highway QC's backed up many of the top gospel stars who played in Chicago, and this exposure gave Sam the opportunity in 1951 to replace retiring tenor Robert Harris in one of the great gospel quartets, the Soul Stirrers. Sam's good looks and smooth style helped him to inspire an immediate following, especially among the young women in his audiences.

The distinctive phrasing and urban enunciation that Sam brought to the sweet soul of gospel helped him to achieve star status. By 1956 the size of his legion of devoted female fans prompted Little Richard's producer "Bumps" Blackwell to approach the Soul Stirrers label, Specialty, about releasing non-gospel songs. Sam recorded several pop songs, releasing "Lovable" under the name Dale Cook, to avoid offending gospel fans. Sam's thinly disguised voice was unmistakable, however, and in an effort to protect the label's large stake in the gospel market, Specialty refused to release any more of "Dale's" tracks.

In 1957, Blackwell arranged for Sam to sign with Keen Records. The new label released "(I Love You) For Sentimental Reasons" and "Lonely

Island," two ballads with a gospel style and secular content. In December, Sam sang "You Send Me," written by his brother Charles, on the *Ed Sullivan Show*. Within a month the single hit number one for two consecutive weeks and charted at number twenty-nine in the UK.

Sam went on to chart ten albums and twenty-nine top-forty singles in the years 1957–1965, including "Wonderful World," "Chain Gang," "Bring It On Home to Me," "Another Saturday Night," and "Little Red Rooster." His vocal style was unique and served as an influence for scores of future stars, including Otis Redding and Wilson Pickett. In 1960 Cooke survived a near fatal air crash, switched to RCA, and developed an interest in music publishing. The following year Sam launched SAR, one of the first artist-owned labels, with J. W. Alexander and manager Roy Crain. One of the first acts they signed was the Soul Stirrers. Just when Sam Cooke's career was expanding and his future looked golden, tragedy struck.

On December 11, 1964, Sam Cooke and a twenty-two-year-old woman checked into a three-dollar room at the Hacienda Motel in south Los Angeles. A few minutes later, the woman ran from the room, pulling on her clothes. Sam followed, wearing only a sports jacket and one shoe, and began pounding on the manager's door, mistakenly thinking the woman was inside. According to the manager, fifty-five-year-old Bertha Lee Franklin, he broke down the door and attacked her. She responded by shooting him three times with a handgun, then pounding him with a broomstick to make sure that he was dead. The death was ruled a justifiable homicide, and though there were rumors of foul play, nothing was ever proven.

The Hacienda, now called the Polaris Motel, is located at 9137 South Figueros in Los Angeles. Sam Cooke is buried in the Court of Freedom section of the Forest Lawn Cemetery, 1712 South Glendale Avenue, Glendale, California.

Marvin Gaye

A longtime king of Motown, Marvin Gaye sang of love, sex, and pain—three never-fail ingredients. With his soulful voice and boundless creativity, Marvin Gaye determined the direction that the Motown sound was to take.

On April 2, 1939, Marvin Gaye was born to the Reverend and Mrs. Gaye. By the time he was five, Marvin was singing in church and traveling to revivals with his father. Although devoutly religious, Reverend Gaye was also a violent man, frequently mentally and physically abusing Marvin. Marvin began to find comfort in music and taught himself to play the piano and the drums. Against his father's wishes, Marvin soon moved from singing in church to singing in a band. When Marvin was a teen, his father began to drink heavily and the beatings worsened. Marvin thought he had finally escaped when he joined the air force in 1955, but when he returned home after an honorable discharge in 1957 his father continued the abuse.

Back at home, Marvin returned to his old defense mechanism—singing—and in 1958 he got his big break when he met Harvey Fuqua. Marvin joined Fuqua's band, the Moonglows, and moved to Chicago. Although the Moonglows broke up after recording a few singles for Chess, Marvin and Harvey moved to Detroit together in 1960.

Once he was in Detroit, it did not take long for Marvin to start working. He played the drums for Smokey Robinson and the Miracles and sang with the Marvelettes before recording his first single, "Let Your Conscience Be Your Guide," for Tamla in 1961. A year later, Marvin released his first hit, "Stubborn Kind of Fellow," followed by "Hitch Hike," and in 1963 made his first appearance on the top-ten chart with "Pride and Joy." Marvin's popularity continued to grow as women all over the world fell under his spell, charmed by his sexy good looks and his versatile, three-octave voice. Motown's Berry Gordy recognized a good thing when he heard it, and though Marvin had always been a little shy, he was soon made Motown's hottest sex symbol. By the end of 1963, he was happily married to Berry's sister, Anna Gordy. Several of his songs are testaments to his love for her, including "Pride and Joy" and "You're a Wonderful One." In the spring of 1964, Marvin recorded "What's the Matter with You, Baby," his first duet with Mary Wells, and established the sensual style that would eventually take him to the top.

Beginning in 1965, Marvin had a series of hits that included "How Sweet It Is (To Be Loved by You)," "I'll Be Doggone," and "It Takes Two," a duet with Kim Weston. In 1967, he found a new partner, Tammi Terrell, aka Thomasina Montgomery.

Born April 29, 1945, in Philadelphia, Thomasina was discovered by Luther Dixon, who signed her to the Scepter/Wand label when she was fifteen. After two singles with Scepter/Wand, Tammi started to record with other labels, releasing "I Cried," which was produced by James Brown on his Try Me label. Following a short, stormy relationship with Brown, Tammi enrolled in the University of Pennsylvania for two years and was married briefly to boxer Ernie Terrell. Then in 1965, Berry Gordy saw Tammi on stage and immediately signed her up, releasing two solo singles before pairing her with Marvin.

The music that Tammi and Marvin made together was truly special. Their voices were a perfect blend of harmony and contrast with an emotional depth so real that many people assumed that they were lovers. In fact, Tammi was in love with David Ruffin and Marvin was fighting to save his marriage. Over the next two years, they released nine top-fifty records, and "Your Precious Love," "Ain't Nothing Like the Real Thing," and "You're All I Need to Get By" made the top ten. In the midst of all this success, Tammi's complaints of headaches were not enough to prepare anyone for the tragedy that was on its way.

In the summer of 1967, the duo was performing at Virginia's Hampton-Sidney College when Tammi suddenly collapsed into Marvin's arms. He carried her offstage and rushed her to a hospital. The doctors found a tumor, and, though Tammi went through surgery eight times, the tumor ultimately proved fatal. She died on March 16, 1970, at Graduate Hospital in Philadelphia, at the age of twenty-four. The shock of the ordeal sent Marvin into seclusion for two years.

In December 1968, "I Heard It Through the Grapevine" became Marvin's first number one hit and the biggest-selling single in Motown's twenty-year history. Marvin had several more hits through 1969, but his personal life did not reflect the professional success. He had never fully recovered from Tammi's death, his marriage was in shambles, and cocaine had become his only joy. At a particularly dark time, Marvin locked himself in his apartment with a loaded gun, threatening to kill himself or anyone who came into the room. He was saved by Pops Gordy (Berry's father), who walked through the door and convinced Marvin to give him the gun. Periods of deep depression and thoughts of suicide haunted Marvin for the rest of his life.

Music kept Marvin going, and he did a lot of

soul searching in his work on *What's Going On*, his masterpiece concept album. This social commentary album was a powerful statement, especially when combined with the raw emotion that was the greatest strength of Marvin's voice. Because of the album's controversial subject matter, Motown did not want to release it. Finally, Marvin gave them an ultimatum: release the album or he would never record for them again. Motown relented and the album was a critical success.

Marvin began preparing for his comeback concert in Washington, D.C. The show was a raging success and officials in the city declared May 1, 1972, Marvin Gaye Day and presented him with a key to the city. Throughout the rest of the seventies, Marvin's career was as erratic as his life. He turned out hits like ''Let's Get It On'' and the caustic ''Here, My Dear,'' a bitter look at his divorce from Anna. The divorce was finalized in 1977 with a settlement that left him nearly bankrupt. Marvin pressed on, and soon he was remarried—to longtime girlfriend Janis Hunter. He divorced his second wife a year later, and his life continued to spiral downward. His drug problem escalated and he began to experiment with freebase.

Marvin's life lost all structure; he lived in the back of a van in Hawaii, and then moved to Europe in order to escape the IRS. Eventually he returned to Los Angeles and moved into the house he had bought for his parents. Marvin had his last moment of glory, finally winning a Grammy for his hit ''Sexual Healing.''

Throughout Marvin's life, his father had been a constant, looming presence. The history of violence, the pent-up resentment, and the heavy drug use finally combined in a deadly Oedipal showdown. On Sunday, April 1, 1984, Marvin hit his father during a violent argument, shoving him out of his bedroom. His father returned moments later with a .38 caliber revolver and shot Marvin point-blank several times in the chest while Mrs. Gaye watched in horror. Marvin was taken to the California Hospital Medical Center and was pronounced dead at 1:01 P.M.

On April 5, over 10,000 people showed up for Marvin's funeral at Forest Lawn Memorial Park, where his band played, Stevie Wonder sang, and Smokey Robinson spoke. Marvin was cremated the next day, and Anna and his three children scattered the ashes in the wind. On September 20, 1984, Marvin's father pleaded no contest to voluntary manslaughter and two months later was sentenced to five years probation.

Since his death, there have been numerous tributes to Marvin, including an induction into the Rock 'n' Roll Hall of Fame in 1987, a star on the Hollywood Walk of Fame in 1990, and a subsequent Motown release of *The Marvin Gaye Collection*, a four-CD set which includes thirty-four previously unreleased tracks.

John Lennon

With the onslaught of the British Invasion, the United States was introduced to perhaps the single greatest rock 'n' roll band in the history of the world. The Beatles defined rock 'n' roll for the decade that they were actively touring and recording, and they continue to do so. John Lennon, the guiding force of the Beatle revolution, left the world with a political and musical message that haunts us to this day.

John Winston Lennon often felt neglected and misunderstood as a child. Soon after John was born on October 9, 1940, his father left the family in Liverpool to join the merchant marines. Over the next several years, John's life was very erratic as he stayed with his free-spirited mother, Julia. Many nights she went out after he fell asleep, leaving him home alone or sending him off to stay with relatives. During these years, John was frequently in trouble at school and often tried to run away. When he was sent to live with his aunt Mimi, he constantly rebelled against her rigid standards of control.

The year John turned fifteen, he heard Elvis sing "Heartbreak Hotel" for the first time. Through the exploration of the world of rock 'n' roll that had been inspired by the American rockabilly of Eddie Cochran, Little Richard, and Jerry Lee Lewis, John found identity and purpose. Although his aunt disapproved of John's new interest, his mother had recently come back into his life and she began to encourage him. Sharing his interest in music, Julia bought John his first guitar and taught him to play. Within a year he started his first group, the Quarrymen, with some friends from the Quarry Bank High School. Guitarist Paul McCartney joined the band in 1957, followed by his old friend George Harrison just a few months later. John quickly recognized a musical counterpart in Paul, and they began to write songs together. The Quarrymen went through several name changes—Johnny and the Moondogs, the Silver Beatles.

Meanwhile, John continued his education at the Liverpool Art College, where he would meet his future wife Cynthia Powell. His roommate at Liverpool was a bass player named Stuart Sutcliffe. Stu was born in Edinburgh, Scotland, on June 23, 1940. In January 1960, Stu became the bassist for the Silver Beatles. The band played extensively throughout Liverpool and Hamburg, Germany, slowly building a loyal following. From August to November of 1960, the Silver Beatles played over 100 shows, with each show lasting as long as eight hours. They finished up the year making their record debut on Polydor as the backup band for Tony Sheridan. Stu left the group in April 1961 to be with his girlfriend, Astria Kircherr.

Nineteen sixty-two was a year of ups and downs for the Silver Beatles. They were turned down by Decca Records in January. A few months later, however, they won top honors in the Mersey Beat popularity poll. The positive turn of events had been brought about in part by a new manager, Brian Epstein, born September 19, 1934, in Liverpool. He cleaned up their image—trading their sweaty leather for an artier, sleeker look—and polished their sound until they were ready to enter the studio.

The band got a contract with EMI/Parlophone in June of '62 and added drummer Ringo Starr in August—their formation was finally complete. The Silver Beatles were in the studio by September, and by October 5, 1962, the group, now just the Beatles, made their record debut with "Love Me Do." Their first offering was a hit, reaching number seventeen in the UK. Their next single, "Please Please Me," did even better, attaining the number two spot in January 1963. February saw their first nationwide tour, and "Beatlemania" began in full force. "From Me to You," the Beatles' next track, went straight to number one and led off a string of eleven consecutive number one hits. This success spread to albums, tours, TV, even their own magazine, and by the end of 1963 the Beatles were indisputably the biggest stars in England. John was also a father; his son Julian had been born considerably less than nine months after John's marriage to Cynthia Powell.

It was January 1964 when the Beatles finally made their U.S. record debut, and their music traveled across the Atlantic without losing any of its strength or popularity. "I Want to Hold Your Hand" was the first that Americans heard of the Beatles, and they wasted no time sending the single to the top of the U.S. charts. In February, the Beatles themselves came to the United States and took the nation by storm with their appearance on the *Ed Sullivan Show*. America adopted the Beatles as her own, welcoming the "British Invasion," and willingly gave the Brits control of the direction of rock 'n' roll for several years. The next two years saw the Beatles rise to unprecedented heights of megastardom.

After two years of relentless touring, screaming teenaged fans, and poppy hits, the Beatles decided to retire from the road. They believed that the public was stifling their creativity, and the group retreated to work on developing their musical vision. *Rubber Soul* was the first fruit of the sequester, in 1965, followed by *Revolver* the year after, and finally their concept album, *Sgt. Pepper's Lonely Hearts Club Band*. These albums combined psychedelia with the haunting sounds of the Indian sitar. Perhaps as important as the eastern influence was the influence of LSD, a drug which, when combined with Lennon's already active imagination, gave birth to a highly experimental flair. In the mid-sixties, the Beatles grew into Epstein's intellectual look, and their music became artistic and thoughtful. The creativity continued into the late sixties, with *The White Album*, *Abbey Road*, and *Let It Be* becoming rallying points for their respective years— '68, '69, and '70.

The end of the sixties marked the effective end of the Beatles. Paul, George, and Ringo went on to film and solo careers, with varying degrees of success. Paul's major post-Beatles accomplishment was, of course, his band Wings. John continued to record, now with new wife Yoko Ono. The duo released *John Lennon/Plastic Ono Band* in 1970 and *Imagine* in 1971, and both albums were testaments to Lennon's genius as well as his angst. The productivity of the early seventies dropped off dramatically, as John's time was taken up by heavy drinking, a crusade for peace, and the fight to maintain his green card. John and Yoko withdrew from the recording scene in the second half of the seventies, but they returned in 1980 with the release of *Double Fantasy*. This comeback album would prove to be Lennon's last.

On the night of December 8, 1980, John Lennon was on his way home from a late recording session when he heard his name being called by a fan, Mark David Chapman. John had given his autograph to Chapman earlier that day, and when he turned to look at him, Chapman fired five shots into John Lennon with a .38 revolver. Lennon arrived at the hospital too late; he was pronounced dead on arrival. As a generation mourned the loss of one of their standard bearers, fans searched for the reason for the crime. Various motivations have been assigned to the assassin—Lennon's remark about Jesus and the Beatles' own popularity, inspiration from the teen-rebellion novel *The Catcher in the Rye*, or a simple quest for attention, but the truth will probably never be known.

One thing we do know is that John Lennon could not be kept down even by death. In 1995, a previously unreleased Beatles single, "Free as a Bird," featured Lennon's unmatchable vocals and rose to the pinnacle of the charts.

Chapter 5

.

Morbid Maladies

Karen Carpenter

Surprisingly, Karen Carpenter made her impression on music, not by riding the rebellion of the sixties, but by asserting traditional values. Always a "good girl" who followed the rules, Karen had a need for acceptance and approval that was just as dangerous as defiance or immoral behavior was for many of her peers. She was born on March 2, 1950, in New Haven, Connecticut, where an early interest in music was sparked by her father's impressive collection of jazz and big band records. Her musical inspiration was her older brother Richard, who was already studying classical piano when the Carpenter family moved to Downey, California, in 1963. Karen decided to follow in his footsteps, so she joined the school marching band and took up the drums.

In 1965, they started their first band, the Carpenter Trio, a three-piece jazz group with Karen on drums and vocals, Richard on keyboards, and Wes Jacobs on bass and tuba. The group had a contract from RCA within a year, the prize they were awarded for winning a major "Battle of the Bands" contest at the Hollywood Bowl. Unfortunately, RCA never released any of their recordings, and the Carpenter Trio broke up before the end of '66.

Karen and Richard took some time off before putting together a new band, Spectrum. When Spectrum split up a short time later, the siblings finally decided to work exclusively as a duo. The Carpenters spent months experimenting with vocal harmonies and the results were impressive. In search of a record deal, they recorded a demo, only to be rejected by company after company.

In April 1969, Herb Alpert of A&M Records decided to take a chance on the duo. Six months later, the Carpenters made their record debut with *Offering*. After a slow start, they released their second album in May of 1970 and its first single took off. The phenomenal success that started with the number one single "(They Long to Be) Close to You" continued with "We've Only Just Begun" and "Rainy Days and Mondays." Their popularity grew as the siblings found a ripe market for their wholesome image and mellow, soft rock sound.

Over the next five years, the Carpenters had fifteen top-forty singles (eleven in the top five), five top-five albums, three Grammies, and their own TV show. Their world tours were consistently sold-out, and a string of their records, including "Superstar," "Top of the World," and "Please Mr. Postman," sold over a million copies.

Everything seemed perfect until the frantic pace of the fast lane took its toll on Karen's health. The first sign of trouble came in 1975, when they were forced to cancel a two-month tour because of her severe exhaustion. The Carpenters took several months off as Karen struggled with anorexia. Her weight had dropped to eighty pounds, and the rest of the seventies was erratic for the duo.

By 1979, Karen struck out on her own artistically, creating music for the first time without her brother, and began recording a solo album in New York. She never finished the record because Richard and A&M convinced her to do another Carpenters album. *Made in America* gave them

one last hit, "Touch Me When I'm Dancing" (number sixteen U.S.), in August of 1981.

Karen's two-year marriage to Thomas Burris was already headed for divorce in 1982, and Karen became too ill to complete another record. After finally acknowledging her anorexia, she spent much of the year in therapy. During treatment, she gained some weight back, allowing her to make public appearances again. She returned with Richard to the studio in early '83 to record *Voices of the Heart*.

But the strain was just too much for her. While visiting her parents in Downey, Karen was sorting through some of her clothes when she collapsed onto the floor of the walk-in closet. She was rushed to Downey Community Hospital, but it was too late. Weakened by years of abuse, her heart gave out at 9:51 A.M. on February 4, 1983. Karen Carpenter had died at the age of thirty-two. Although cardiac arrest due to anorexia was recorded as the official cause of death, certain people claim that Karen's persistent use of Ipecac, a substance used to induce vomiting, had overwhelmed her system.

Richard finished the Carpenters last album, *Voices of the Heart*, by October 1983 and dedicated it to his sister. There have been several greatest hits albums, a box set, and a well-received TV movie, *The Karen Carpenter Story*.

Eric Carr

KISS, perhaps the ultimate glam rock band of the seventies and early eighties, made a name for themselves with their loud music, loud makeup, and unapologetic flamboyance. Seldom seen in public without full makeup, KISS remained enigmatic in many ways throughout their two-decade tenure in the rock 'n' roll mainstream. KISS was one of the pioneers of stadium rock, and their elaborate stage shows were as important to the image as was their slamming beat and wild guitars.

Eric Carr was with KISS for eleven years, and during his time with the band he saw it grow and evolve beyond his wildest expectations. KISS started out as a trio, the outgrowth of the second incarnation of Wicked Lester. The first Wicked Lester had recorded but had never released a hard-edged debut album and they folded when the Epic label dropped them from the roster. Paul Stanley, on rhythm guitar and vocals, and Gene Simmons, on bass and vocals, were undaunted by Wicked Lester's initial failure and determined to continue in the music industry. They sang backup vocals on Lyn Christopher's solo debut album before deciding to reinvent Wicked Lester. It was 1972 and they needed a drummer.

Meanwhile, Peter Criss, a feisty drummer, was looking for work. His band, Lips, had just dissolved, and he put an advertisement in *Rolling Stone* magazine:

Drummer with eleven years' experience will do anything to make it.

Simmons and Stanley responded to the ad and hired Criss on the spot, and the trio began rehearsing on West 23rd Street in a freezing cold Manhattan loft. They changed their name to KISS and advertised in the *Village Voice* for the final ingredient, a guitarist:

Wanted: a guitarist with flash.

Their flashy guitarist appeared in the form of Ace Frehley, the sixty-first person to audition. He wore one orange sneaker and one red sneaker, and he wowed the trio with his skill and innovation. After his callback, the group was sold and KISS became a complete quartet.

It is perhaps appropriate to the genre of glam rock that KISS put together a promo kit before recording even a single. The kit included a series of color photos, some of the few to be taken without makeup. On January 30, 1973, KISS played its first show, at the Popcorn club in New York City. The three-show series was not a success monetarily (the group earned a total of seventy dollars). Nor did the group begin to build any sort of following (Gene's girlfriend, her brother, and the bartender were the only audience members on opening night). The gig was significant, however, because it was the night that the KISS concept—the makeup and the logo—was born.

In the next three months, KISS embarked on the trail to fame that would last well into the next decade. They attracted attention for their appearance but also for their tight sound, and soon they were selling out New York clubs every weekend. In June of 1973, KISS recorded several singles: "Strutter," "Deuce," "Watching You," "Black Diamond," and "Cold Gin" in the Electric Lady Studios. These demo-singles were not released, but four months later the band finally began recording an album, *Kiss*, that was destined to end up in the record stores. That year closed with a New Year's Eve show at the NYC Academy of Music, during which Gene lit his hair on fire during a fire-breathing act. He recovered quickly.

KISS toured extensively in 1974, performing both on their own and as opening acts. They recorded a second album which, like the first one, failed to chart but delighted the growing number of dedicated KISS fans. The third album, *Dressed to Kill*, was released early in 1975 and contained the first KISS top-100 single. "Rock and Roll All Night" reached number sixty-four in May of 1975. Later that month, KISS played to its first sellout arena—Cobo Hall in Detroit, Michigan. The May tour yielded the *KISS Alive!* album, and the live version of "Rock and Roll All Night" reached number twelve on the charts. The album eventually went gold.

With recording and performance successes under their belts, KISS was unstoppable. *Destroyer*, released in 1976, became KISS' second gold album, and May of the same year saw KISS cross the Atlantic for the first time. The European tour was followed up with an equally successful American tour, and KISS came up with their first top-ten single two months later. "Beth," released in August, reached number seven on September 25. The year of 1976 ended in much the same way that 1973 did—Gene set his hair on fire once again, having failed to master the fire-breathing stunt entirely. All told, Gene would set his hair on fire seven times during his career.

The hits kept coming, and KISS became the only group in 1977 to score three platinum albums. They were named number two on the Billboard artist of the year chart and number one in a Gallup Youth Survey. KISS ended 1977 with three sellout performances in Madison Square Garden, and no one set his hair on fire. In 1978 KISS expanded into other media as they starred in the NBC made-for-TV movie, *KISS Meets the Phantom of the Park*. By the end of the following year, the KISS lineup was about to change as Peter Criss began to make noises about leaving the group.

Criss' departure marked the end of an era but certainly not the end of KISS. He was replaced by Eric Carr, a young fireball with little performing experience but endless talent and energy. Carr decided on a fox for his makeup persona and the transition was complete. Soon after Carr joined the band, they embarked on a highly profitable European tour followed by a blockbuster trek through Australia. By the end of the touring marathon, Eric was firmly ensconced as a senior member of the band, and in July of 1981 he and Gene flew to Vienna to receive a People's Choice award.

This Vienna junket was a brief intermission in KISS' ferocious recording schedule, the result of which was KISS' only concept album, *Music from the Elder*. *Elder* received critical acclaim but little commercial success, and KISS performed only one show in support of the album. While working on the next album, Ace Frehley crashed his car and withdrew from active participation in the group. He toured with KISS in October of 1982, but in November Ace announced that he was resigning from the band.

Ace was replaced by Vinnie Vincent, leaving only two of the original four band members on the scene. The year 1983 marked another major change as well, for June 25 was the date of the final performance done in makeup. KISS appeared on MTV without makeup for the first time on September 18, and in December they were named the loudest band in the world. After several altercations, Vinnie left the group in March of 1984 and was replaced by Mark St. John, who was subsequently replaced by Bruce Kulick. Kulick was broken in during the 1985 *Animalize* tour and accompanying full-length video. Countless successes followed, both from the recording studio and the video camera. Fifteen years of KISS was celebrated in November of 1988 with the release of a greatest hits album, *Smashes, Thrashes and Hits*. Eric Carr was featured in a new version of "Beth" as well as the brand-new controversial single, "Let's Put the X In Sex." The album went platinum in a matter of weeks.

The next two years were a roller-coaster for KISS. After a year of exhausting touring and recording, the band released its first top-ten hit in fourteen years. "Forever" hit number eight in February, and KISS appeared to be on the verge of a winning streak. Their fortune reversed, however, and the bad luck began in June when Paul Stanley cracked several ribs on stage by running into a metal bar. The following month, Stanley was involved in another accident, this time totaling his car.

The real tragedy struck in 1991, when a tumor was discovered in Eric Carr's heart. He underwent surgery in April, but his case proved terminal. Millions of KISS fans learned in August that their beloved drummer was battling cancer and would no longer be able to play with the band. In September, Eric suffered a brain aneurysm and the final struggle began. Eric's fight ended on November 24, 1991, when he passed away. In true KISS fashion, the band played on, dedicating their next album, *Revenge*, to Eric's memory. Eric Singer replaced Eric Carr on the drums, but Carr continued to live in the hearts of the fans.

Woody Guthrie

Woody Guthrie was writing folk-rock protest ballads before most of the protest singers of the sixties picked up a guitar. Fortunately, his genius did not go unnoticed, and today many of the biggest names in folk and rock hail Woody Guthrie as their greatest influence.

Woodrow Wilson Guthrie was born in Okemah, Oklahoma, on July 14, 1912. His father was a singer, banjo player, and semipro boxer who instilled in Woody a lifelong love of music. Woody left home at the age of sixteen and took jobs in Texas and Louisiana as a newsboy, sign painter, spittoon washer, and farm laborer. As he searched for a niche, Woody took to singing in the streets. In 1929, his uncle taught him to play the guitar, and with his new skill Woody hopped a freight train and began to ride the rails. His instrument made him a favorite among the hobos, and Woody did not retire from the gypsy lifestyle until 1937. When he finally did decide to settle down, Woody Guthrie moved to Los Angeles and worked at a local radio station, hosting a radio show for one dollar a day.

As he matured, Woody discovered a strong liberal political streak in himself and moved to New York City at the outbreak of World War II. He flirted briefly with communism but was turned away from the party when he refused to give up his religion. He joined the merchant marines instead, winning many fans within the ranks for his antifascist songs. Guthrie was stationed in England, Italy, and Africa during his three-year tour of duty, and when he returned to the U.S., he continued to write songs about the injustice that he saw in the world.

It was during the 1940's that Woody Guthrie wrote his most famous songs—"This Land Is Your Land," "Pastures of Plenty," "So Long, It's Been Good to Know You" were among the most popular of his hundreds of compositions. His lyrics cut at the evils of the establishment, but because his subtle irony was often lost on the majority of his listeners, Guthrie's songs were often misunderstood. The sharper of his fans, especially fellow songwriters, grasped Guthrie's meaning and wit and gave him the respect that his creations deserved.

The years on the rails that had given Woody his insight and perspective had also left him with a debilitating alcohol dependency. In 1952, he was diagnosed as an alcoholic and confined to a mental institution. It turned out that alcoholism was not the worst of his problems. After a few years of institutionalization, Woody was correctly diagnosed with Huntington's disease, a genetic degenerative disorder of the nervous system. This disease, which had killed his mother, disabled Woody for the last decade of his life. His hospital visitors included Bob Dylan, one of his biggest fans.

Woody Guthrie's suffering ended on October 3, 1967, in Queens, New York, but his memory did not die. Lifelong friend Pete Seeger organized a series of memorial concerts in the late sixties. Two of these shows, at Carnegie Hall in 1968 and the Hollywood Bowl in 1970, were recorded and released as successful albums. The shows featured performances by Bob Dylan, Tom Paxton, Joan Baez, Judy Collins, Richie Havens, and Country Joe McDonald. In 1976, Guthrie's life story was made into a major motion picture, *Bound for Glory*. Woody Guthrie's music lived on in one final way— his son Arlo became a singer-songwriter, following in the pioneering footsteps of his beloved father.

Freddie Mercury

Freddie Mercury was the voice of Queen, a band that helped to define the seventies by delivering a peculiar vision laced with the elements of hard rock. Mercury and Queen epitomized the decade's curious combination of jaded opulence and childish playfulness.

Born Frederick Bulsara in Zanzibar on September 5, 1946, Freddie Mercury was raised in Bombay, India, before moving to England with his parents in 1959. Although he lived less than 100 yards from future band mate Brian May, the two would not meet until 1970. The son of a government accountant, Freddie earned a degree in graphic design at Ealing College of Art. It was around this time that he became a vocalist for an unrecorded blues-rock group called Wreckage and became friendly with members of Smile, a power band featuring guitarist May and drummer Roger Meadows-Taylor. When Smile split up, Mercury, May, and Taylor started a new band which Freddie christened Queen. Bassist John Deacon was recruited through a classified ad, and the lineup that would remain intact for two decades was complete.

Queen played clubs and colleges for almost two years while the members maintained their lives outside the group—May and Taylor both pursued advanced degrees. In 1972 Queen was given the opportunity to make a demo tape in exchange for showcasing new recording hardware at De-Lane Lea Studios. The engineers present were impressed and they suggested to their employers, Trident Audio Productions, that the group be signed to a management deal. Trident agreed, and then pitched the demo to EMI which signed Queen to a recording contract.

In June 1973, while awaiting the launch of Queen's first album, Freddie released a cover of the Beach Boys' "I Can Hear Music." In July, EMI released Queen's eponymous album and debut single, "Keep Yourself Alive." The album and the single both went unnoticed by the listening public. A tour followed, opening for Mott the Hoople, and finally Queen began to gain some recognition.

Particular attention was given to Freddie's shrill lead vocals and May's flamboyant guitar style that prompted comparisons to Led Zeppelin. In 1974, the eclectic *Queen II* and the single "Seven Seas of Rhye" both made the charts in the UK.

Queen embarked on a tour in support of their album, and they soon made their television debut on *Top of the Pops*. This TV appearance was the result of a lucky break when David Bowie's promo film was unavailable and Queen had to fill in. Queen's exposure on the show had a huge impact on the music industry, and the band was on its way to the top. Later that year, a third album, *Sheer Heart Attack*, became a hit, and the singles "Killer Queen" and "Now I'm Here" introduced the band to America.

The year 1975 saw the release of *A Night at the Opera*, the album which gave us "Bohemian Rhapsody." This innovative single topped the British charts for nine straight weeks. Featuring Freddie's over-the-top rock operatic style, the single was unique also because of its length (5:22). The accompanying film helped to spawn the industry trend of producing videos to promote records.

Queen continued to ride a wave of enormous popularity, cranking out hits like "We Are the Champions," "We Will Rock You," "Crazy Little Thing Called Love," and "Another One Bites the Dust." As the eighties progressed, however, the band developed an image problem. Freddie cut his hair and grew a mustache, and there was widespread speculation that he was gay. Others said he was just trying to look gay because it was trendy. The backlash intensified in 1984 when Freddie dressed as a housewife in the video for "I Want To Be Free." Queen defended the video as typical British humor, and though it was popular in England, many Americans missed the joke. The band also took its licks by playing in Sun City, South Africa, a move which Freddie justified shamelessly by saying, "There's a lot of money to be made." It was a move that landed Queen on the United Nations blacklist.

As the eighties progressed, the band began to lose momentum as members broke away to do solo projects. Freddie recorded "Love Kills" on Giorgio Moroder's new soundtrack for the silent film *Metropolis* and released a solo album, *Mr. Bad Guy*. Then a show-stealing performance at the 1985 Live Aid benefit catapulted both Freddie and Queen back into favor as they blew away the likes of Paul McCartney, Bob Dylan, and a reunited Led Zeppelin. Organizer Bob Geldof labeled the event "the perfect stage for Freddie. He could pounce in front of the whole world . . ." Brian May recalled, "The rest of us played okay, but Freddie was out there and took it to another level. It wasn't just Queen fans. He connected with everyone."

Though he continued to record with Queen, Freddie spent the rest of the decade involved in a variety of other projects as well, including a duet with Spanish opera singer Monserrat Caballe which reached number eight on the UK charts.

On November 23, 1991, Freddie went public with the fact that had been the subject of vast speculation for over two years. He was dying of AIDS. To the press, which mobbed the gate of his Edwardian mansion in London's Kensington district, he issued a written statement: "I felt it correct to keep the information private to date in order to protect the privacy of those around me. However, the time has now come for my friends and fans around the world to know the truth, and I hope that everyone will join me, my doctors, and all those worldwide in the fight against this terrible disease."

The statement proved to be Freddie's last farewell to the world, for the day after it was is-sued, Freddie Mercury was dead and his body cremated. The following April, 72,000 fans gave Freddie a posthumous send-off at Wembly Stadium. The memorial was called the Concert for Life, and it was rock 'n' roll's first major rallying cry in the fight against AIDS. The concert featured performances by a huge diversity of talent, including Elton John, David Bowie, Annie Lennox, Axl Rose, George Michael, and the surviving members of Queen. The event attracted approximately one billion television viewers worldwide and is estimated to have raised up to $35 million for AIDS care and education.

Frank Zappa

Through music, Frank Zappa found a way to make meaningful commentary on the state of the world and its values. His mixed bag of rock 'n' roll and biting wit led many of his fans—and enemies—down the road of intellectual discourse and self-examination.

Zappa was born in 1940 in Baltimore, Maryland, near the Arsenal Army Chemical Center. His father studied the effects of weather on the gasses and explosions of chemical warfare. Frank grew up, therefore, around evidence of the destructive powers of the military-industrial complex, and the memory of it would stay with him all of his life. Due in part to young Frank's poor health, the family relocated several times—to Florida and then to Lancaster, California. In the midst of a fairly uprooted childhood, Frank Zappa turned to music. He enjoyed Spike Jones' parodies of famous people, and he worshipped the blues greats: Slim Harpo, Howlin' Wolf, Lightnin' Slim, Muddy Waters, Joe Houston, and Sonny Boy Williamson. He began to make his own music in high school, first as a percussionist in the school band. After Zappa was kicked out of the band for smoking, he founded a rhythm and blues outfit which he called the Black-Outs.

Determined to make a life out of music, Zappa began to look for work in the industry after he graduated from high school. While on the search, he worked as a greeting card designer, a copywriter, a window dresser, and a jewelry salesman. His break came when a former English teacher and aspiring screenwriter, Don Cerveris, helped Zappa secure the job of composing the soundtrack for the 1964 release of the film *Run Home Slow*. Later that same year, Zappa became the rhythm guitarist for a band called the Soul Giants. Soon he began to contribute his experimental compositions, and the band was intrigued by their alternating time signatures and irregular patterns. Beyond the musical innovations, Zappa introduced the humorous element of parody into the music, in a reaction against the self-importance he saw in many rock musicians.

The quirky Soul Giants were by all accounts an underground band, but they nonetheless assembled quite a following in the Los Angeles club scene. In 1965, the Soul Giants became the Mothers——and signed a record deal with MGM. *Freak Out* was released and the band became known as Mothers of Invention, in order to erase the ob-

scene implications of the earlier name. The album has the distinction of being the first concept album, with each song being a comment on a societal ill. "Hungry Freaks Daddy" attacked the mediocrity of the educational system. "Trouble Coming Every Day" cried out against racism. The album received little airtime, but rumor has it that it was one of the inspirations for the Beatles' *Sgt. Pepper's Lonely Hearts Club Band*.

Zappa and the Mothers continued to record, exhibiting their musical and conceptual versatility with the melodic offering *Absolutely Free* and the technical, orchestral *Lumpy Gravy*. Zappa mocked the hypocrisy that he saw in the hippie movement and expressed his disgust in the satirical single, "We're Only in It for the Money." His disdain for the hippies extended to his own fans, and in 1969 Zappa dissolved the Mothers because he refused to continue "playing for people who clap for all the wrong reasons."

Frank worked solo for a while, making several noteworthy recordings, before he reassembled a new version of the Mothers of Invention. The new group was dedicated to the ideal of "invention" and began the practice of setting stories to music. The stage performances of these creations flirted with performance art, utilizing rotten vegetables, animalistic sound effects, rude gestures, as well as Zappa's ever-growing guitar virtuosity. Zappa's next project was *200 Motels*, his film production debut which starred Ringo Starr as Zappa.

Over the next few years, Frank Zappa traveled the globe, touring and sharing his biting humor and musical creativity. He founded a record company and released his *Apostrophe*, another concept, narrative album about an Eskimo named Nanook. Zappa's works that followed became increasingly avant-garde and atonal while maintaining a high degree of musical integrity. In the process, he made plenty of enemies, in the music industry and in politics, but he also developed a growing hoard of devoted fans, who anxiously awaited each new release. The year 1982 saw the release of a commercially successful album, *Ship Arriving Too Late to Save a Drowning Witch.* "Valley Girls," a hit single from the album, featured his daughter Moon Unit's teenage voice. Zappa's other children were named Dweezil, Diva, and Ahmet Rodin.

In a testament to his versatility, Zappa turned from "Valley Girls" to a recording session of his orchestral pieces with the London Symphony Orchestra. While the project was not a commercial success, it earned him a name in classical circles, and Zappa compositions began to appear in symphony halls throughout the world. From classical, Zappa moved to explore the jazz idiom, and in 1986 he was awarded a Grammy for his breakthrough album, *Jazz From Hell.*

Throughout his career, Zappa kept up an active involvement in politics, fighting the restriction of artistic expression wherever he saw it. A registered Democrat, Zappa was actually rather conservative and often said that he would switch parties if it were not for the moralizing restrictions of the religious right. He testified at a congressional hearing against Tipper Gore's clean music crusade, calling it a violation of the First Amendment. In 1990, Czechoslovakia's president, Václav Havel, invited Zappa to serve as a trade representative to the fledgling democracy. Havel, a dissident poet under the Communist regime, saw Zappa as an inspirational force for the Czech people. Havel was forced to revoke the invitation after receiving pressure from Secretary of State James Baker, whose wife served on Tipper Gore's Parents Music Resource Center.

Frank Zappa was a man with a mission, a drive to make the world a freer, more open-minded place. In 1991 that mission became an urgent one when Zappa was diagnosed with terminal prostate cancer. With the end in sight, he continued to work feverishly, fourteen hours a day, often in intense pain. He had so many songs, so many ideas yet to be put to paper, and he knew he was working against the clock. On December 4, 1993, Frank Zappa's time ran out and he passed away. He left hours of recordings, still unreleased, the embodiment of his eternal creativity and dedication to music and to the human mind.

Chapter 6

.

Life in the Fast Lane

Jesse Belvin

Jesse Belvin's "Earth Angel" has come to the spotlight again and again, covered by various artists in various settings. Belvin made many other contributions to the evolution of rhythm and blues as well, and one can only imagine the impact he could have had if he had lived longer.

On December 15, 1933, Jesse Belvin was born in Texarkana, Arkansas. Soon thereafter, his family moved out to central Los Angeles. There, Jesse joined the church choir at the age of seven and quickly discovered the power of gospel music. Jesse was just sixteen and still a student at Jefferson High School when he got his start as a singer in Big Jay McNeely's band. In 1951, Jesse made his recording debut with the band and then went on to turn out several solo offerings over the next two years. Between solo projects, Jesse continued to sing with the band until 1953, when he joined the U.S. Army and was transferred to Germany. During his time overseas, Jesse and two

Army buddies wrote "Earth Angel," the classic song that would become a million-seller for the Penguins (1954), a top-ten hit for the Crew-Cuts (1955), and a top-ten hit for Paul Anka (1969).

After his tour of duty, Jesse returned to Los Angeles and started a duo with Marvin Phillips called Jesse and Marvin. They produced a top-ten R&B hit, "Dream Girl," on Specialty Records, catapulting Jesse into the Los Angeles R&B scene. He began to help local bands by writing songs, working out vocal arrangements, and finding sponsors. Jesse continued to record solo work, as well as group productions under such names as the Cliques (actually Jesse's voice recorded four times), the Sharptones, and the Shields, which had a hit version of "You Cheated" on Dot Records. Throughout the fifties, Jesse released songs on fifteen different labels.

In 1956, Jesse signed with Modern Records and released "Goodnight My Love," another top-ten hit and his biggest success as a singer. The record's success was due partly to disc jockey Alan Freed, who liked the song so much that he used it as the closing theme for his New York radio show. Jesse's wife, JoAnn, became his manager, and in late 1958 she secured him a new contract with RCA Records. Jesse released several records,

and his biggest RCA hit, ''Guess Who'' (cowritten with wife JoAnn), was his last.

After making such lasting contributions to the rock 'n' roll canon, Jesse was destined for an early exit. On February 6, 1960, Jesse was on his way home from a performance in Little Rock, Arkansas, when his car ran off the road. He and his wife were both killed in the crash.

Marc Bolan

As standard-bearers of 1970's rock 'n' roll, T. Rex ruled the British charts for half a decade. They receded from the mainstream as the seventies wore on, but the craze known as ''T. Rextasy'' left its mark as a fan network that approached cult status.

Mark Feld was born on September 30, 1947, in London, England. As a young boy, Mark received Bill Haley's ''Rock Around the Clock,'' and the record inspired Mark to learn to play the guitar. Soon Mark was hooked on rock 'n' roll, and by the age of fifteen, he was immersed in London's ''mod'' scene.

Influenced by singers like Donovan, Mark

changed his name to Toby Tyler and started singing in London's folk clubs. In November 1965, Toby signed a short-term contract with Decca Records and debuted with an unsuccessful single, ''The Wizard.'' After one more unsuccessful single, Toby was dropped from Decca Records. In late 1966, however, Parlophone allowed him to record ''Hippy Gumbo.'' When this too failed, Toby joined a band called Toby's Children which recorded a few singles before breaking up.

In 1967, Toby and percussionist Steve Peregrine Took (born July 28, 1949) formed Tyrannosaurus Rex, an acoustic duo. Toby changed his name again, this time to Marc Bolan. Marc's fascination with magic, fantasy, and mythology was often reflected in the duo's lyrics. By the spring of '68 they made their record debut on EMI with the single "Debora" reaching UK number thirty-four. The first album, *My People Were Fair and had Sky in Their Hair, But Now They're Content to Wear Stars on Their Brow*, was released a few months later and reached number fifteen on the British charts. The duo released another LP and three singles, building a loyal but narrow following. Took was not satisfied with the duo's limited success, and he left in '69 after a mediocre first tour of the U.S.

Marc decided to replace Took with Mickey Finn, and the new combination attained the success that had eluded the old one. Marc started playing electric guitar and shortened the new duo's name to T. Rex. For the next few years, T. Rex was on top of the world with a long string of hits including "Jeepster," "Hot Love," and "Telegram Sam." All of these releases spent time at number one in the UK. Topping the British charts for four weeks, "Bang a Gong (Get It On)" was also their biggest American hit, reaching U.S. number ten in early '72. By the end of 1972 there were several more hits, including singles "Metal Guru" (UK number one), "Children of the Revolution" (UK number two), "Solid Gold Easy Action" (UK number three), and album *The Slider* (UK number four/U.S. number seventeen).

While T. Rex's records were topping the charts, their adoring fans were causing near riots at every performance. This worldwide hysteria,

known as T. Rextasy or T. Rex Mania, became the subject of a movie, *Born to Boogie*, directed by Ringo Starr. Sadly, the decline of T. Rex had already begun when the movie came out in 1973. They continued to tour and record, but the glory days faded until T. Rex finally broke up in 1975. Although Marc never regained his former fame, he continued to record on his own and in 1976 he started a new T. Rex. The revival never got off the ground, however, and in 1977 Marc was hosting his own TV show, *Marc*, and writing for an English pop magazine. Just as his comeback started to take off, however, it came to a tragic end.

On September 16, 1977, Marc and his girlfriend, singer Gloria Jones, were driving home after a late night of London nightclubs. It was approximately five A.M. when Gloria lost control of the mini on a dangerous bend in the road on Barnes Common. The car left the road and hit a tree, killing Marc just weeks before his thirtieth birthday.

Marc's contributions to the music world continued after his death. *Crimson Moon* was released eight months after the accident, in April 1978. It was the first of a series of records which continued for over a decade after Marc's death and which included the number-five hit, *Best of the 20th Century Boy*, released in May 1985. The end of the eighties saw the release of his TV appearances on video and the CD release of his LP's, all of which served as evidence of Marc Bolan's enduring popularity.

Cliff Burton

Although Metallica broke into the heavy metal scene in 1981 as part of the "new wave" of heavy metal, they truly came into their own when they branched off to pursue the relentless pace and heavy rhythms of speed metal. Bassist Cliff Burton was responsible in large part for the signature beat and heavy feel of the Metallica sound.

Growing up in San Francisco, Burton got his first break with a local band known as Trauma. Meanwhile, a band was starting up in L.A. with drummer Lars Ulrich, vocalist/guitarist James Hetfield, guitarist Dave Mustaine, and bassist Ron McGovney. In October of 1981, this fledgling group recorded a single, "Hit the Lights," with virtually no public reaction. Refusing to give up, the unnamed band pressed on and recorded a seven-track demo that they called "No Life Till Leather" and received the same response. McGovney became frustrated by the sluggish start and quit the band after the second failure. It was then that Ulrich discovered Burton playing with Trauma.

Burton was reluctant to leave Trauma and San Francisco, so Ulrich offered the compromise of moving Metallica to San Francisco. After four months of indecision, Cliff Burton decided to make the switch. Soon after Burton climbed aboard, Metallica relocated again, this time to New Jersey. They were in search of a record contract, and in March of 1983 they signed with the Megaforce label. Before they could begin recording, the lineup changed once again when Mustaine left to pursue a solo career. He was quickly replaced by Kirk Hammet, and in May Metallica began recording *Kill 'Em All*. The debut album was released in May of 1983 in the United Kingdom under the Music for Nations Label. Metallica followed it up with a successful British tour with Raven, but *Kill 'Em All* did not reach American audiences.

Metallica burst into the American market the next year, with *Ride the Lightning*, released under first the Megaforce label and then Elektra. This second offering took Metallica into the realm of "speed metal" or "thrash metal." Pioneers in this area, Metallica brought the movement to the attention of the American mainstream and charted at the number 100 spot in the U.S. The album went to number eighty-seven in Britain.

By August of 1985, Metallica was firmly established as a formidable power in heavy metal, playing to a sellout crowd at the Monsters of Rock heavy metal festival at Castle Donnington, Liecs. *Master of Puppets*, released in March of 1986, put the band into the top forty in the U.S., though the album included no hit singles. It was successful enough to win them an American tour with Ozzy Osbourne, in spite of the fact that the band had not enlisted the aid of MTV. After the American tour, Metallica was finally able to release their first album, *Kill 'Em All*, in the United States, where it reached number 155.

From the U.S. tour, Metallica went directly on to a European tour, which proved to be equally successful. Successful, that is, until tragedy struck. On September 27, 1986, Metallica finished up a blockbuster Swedish show and boarded their tour bus to head to the next gig. The Swedish show ended up being the last of the tour. An hour after departure, the tour bus ran off the road, crashed, and killed Cliff Burton instantly. The rest of the band escaped unscathed, though emotionally crushed. Metallica canceled the remaining shows and returned to San Francisco for a memorial service.

Harry Chapin

H arry Chapin's overwhelming compassion lent an urgency to his otherwise sentimental folk ballads. He was concerned for his fellow human beings and was proud to wear his heart on his sleeve.

Harry Chapin was born into a musical family on December 7, 1942, in New York City's Greenwich Village. Playing music was an ambition that started with Harry's father, Jim, a swing drummer who played with both Tommy Dorsey and Woody Herman. Harry's brothers, Tom and Steve, both played in various bands as well, and Harry followed their lead, learning to play the trumpet, the guitar, and the banjo. Harry made his debut public appearance as a young singer with the Brooklyn Heights Boys Choir. It was there that he made the acquaintance of Robert Lamm, who would later rock the charts with his group Chicago.

Encouraged by the growing folk music scene, Harry soon put together an act with his brothers. They covered the folk hits of the day, playing sporadically throughout Harry's college years at the Air Force Academy. Displaying his multifaceted personality, Harry trained as a pilot and studied architecture and philosophy at Cornell. In 1964, Harry left Cornell to join his father and brothers in a group called the Chapin Brothers. The family performed at a variety of Greenwich Village clubs before recording their first album, *Chapin Music*, for Rockland Records. The group disbanded the next year when Tom and Steve returned to school.

Harry had other plans, and on November 26, 1968, he married Sandy Cashmore, a divorced mother of three. Realizing that he needed steady work to support this ready-made family, Harry turned his attention to filmmaking. He worked his way up from film packer to editor to director of his own movies by the late 1960's. In 1969 he received an Academy Award nomination for *The Legendary Champions*, the boxing documentary he made with Jim Jacobs.

While working on his next film, Harry decided to make a serious commitment to music, and in 1970 he gave up film and began to write songs for the reunited Chapins. By 1971, Harry and his brothers had put together "Harry," a new folk-rock band that included acoustic guitar and cello.

Harry opted for the nontraditional route of self-promotion and rented New York's Village Gate for a summer concert run.

Well received by both critics and the public, Harry was courted by six major labels. When they finally signed with Elektra Records in November of 1971, Harry's nine-album deal was the biggest new artist contract in the company's twenty-year history. In June of 1972, Harry's debut album *Heads and Tales* reached number sixty on the U.S. album charts and contained the hit single "Taxi." "Taxi" was a surprise success because of its length—almost seven minutes. Harry found a ticket to success—he had a storytelling style that set him apart from most of the popular confessional and soul-searching folk artists of the time.

Harry's sentimental style earned him a substantial audience that greatly appreciated hits like "W*O*L*D" and "Cat's in the Cradle," which reached number one on the pop charts in 1974. Even with recording and a tireless tour schedule, Harry found time for other projects, including the experimental Broadway revue, *The Night That Made America Famous*, which was nominated for two Tony awards. It was also at this time that he turned his attention to the epidemic problem of world hunger. He cofounded WHY (World Hunger Year), an organization which staged benefit concerts to combat global famine.

Although Harry's record sales had begun to decline by the late seventies, his popularity remained strong and he maintained a hectic international touring schedule. He remained dedicated to the fight against hunger, and at least half of his 200 annual concerts were benefits. Following the release of the album *Sequel* in late 1980, Harry's recording career took off once again. The album peaked at U.S. number fifty-eight and the title track was a sequel to "Taxi" and climbed the charts to number twenty-three.

Although he sang about it, driving had never been one of Harry's fortes. After several accidents and numerous tickets, Harry's driver's license was revoked, but he continued driving illegally. Then, on July 17, 1981, his car was rear-ended by a tractor-trailer on the Long Island Expressway near Jericho, New York. The collision ruptured his gas tank and moments later the car exploded. The exact cause of death is unknown, though an autopsy revealed that he may have suffered a heart attack either before or after the crash.

Harry Chapin is buried at the Huntington Rural Cemetery in Huntington, New York. A memorial fund in his honor was started with a $10,000 donation from Elektra and on December 7, 1987, Chapin was honored with a special Congressional Gold Medal for his work. In 1990, the Relativity label released a tribute album that included the memorial service and several live concert recordings.

Eddie Cochran

Eddie Cochran was a young talent whose spirited guitar and vocal compositions earned him a place among the founding fathers of the rockabilly sound. Although he only released one album before his life was cut short, his influence is felt by countless country, rock, and punk artists.

Ray Edward "Eddie" Cochran was born October 3, 1938, in Oklahoma City, Oklahoma, but his family soon moved to Albert Lee, Minnesota. Listening to the country-western station was Eddie's first experience with music, and country music became a major influence on his future "rockabilly" style. At the age of twelve, Eddie convinced his parents to buy him a guitar, and he lost no time in teaching himself how to play it.

By the time the Cochrans moved to Bell Gardens, California, in 1953, Eddie was already a proficient guitar player. He soon formed his own band, a country trio called the Cochran Brothers. It was at a local show that Eddie met songwriter Jerry Capeheart, who later became his cowriter, manager, and producer. The Cochran Brothers made demos of a few of the Cochran/Capeheart tunes and the tracks went into their first—and last—album.

The Cochran Brothers broke up soon after their recording debut, but Eddie and Jerry remained together, moving between Los Angeles and Nashville as they wrote their songs. Their first break turned out to be Eddie's movie debut in *The Girl Can't Help It*, a rock movie classic. Even though Eddie had only a small cameo appearance, his singing "Twenty Flight Rock" made quite an impression. Liberty Records signed him and his singles did moderately well over the next few years. It wasn't until 1958, however, that Eddie found his personal formula for success. "Summertime Blues" was a rockin' teen anthem that hit number eight on the charts and went gold. It would prove to be Eddie's only top-ten hit. Eddie followed up this initial success with several more lesser hits, including "C'mon Everybody" and "Somethin' Else" (cowritten with Sharon Sheeley). Cochran and his band, the Kelly Four, continued to maintain a rigorous touring schedule in the midst of all this recording.

By the beginning of 1960, everything was falling into place: Eddie had just finished recording *Three Steps to Heaven* and he was about to begin his first UK tour, with Gene Vincent sharing the bill. Eddie was already a huge star in England, and the UK tour was a triumph. In March of 1960, Eddie invited his fiancée, songwriter Sharon Sheeley, to join him for the last few weeks of the tour.

Following the last show, Eddie, Sharon, and Gene Vincent hired a car to drive them to London so they could catch an early flight to the U.S. It was early April 17, 1960, when they left the Bristol Hippodrome in the rented Ford Consul driven by nineteen-year-old George Martin. They were less than halfway to the city when a tire blew out on the A4 near Chippenham, Wiltshire, and Martin lost control of the car. The car crashed into a lamppost, Eddie was thrown through the windshield, and Vincent and Sharon were both injured. Rushed to the hospital, Eddie never regained consciousness. At four P.M., Eddie Cochran died from severe head injuries. He was twenty-one years old.

The numerous posthumous honors started just one month after Eddie's death with the release of his album, appropriately titled *Three Steps to Heaven*. In 1963 a tribute record called *Just Like Eddie* was released, and in 1980 a limited edition box set of Eddie's hits was released. Eddie Cochran was inducted into the Rock 'n' Roll Hall of Fame in 1983. In addition to the formal recognition, Eddie received praise from his colleagues in the form of imitation. The Rolling Stones, the Stray Cats, Debbie Harry, and the Sex Pistols are among the countless artists who have covered Eddie's songs over the years.

Pete De Freitas

Although Echo and the Bunnymen made an innovative impact on the British rock 'n' roll scene in the early eighties, they failed to transport their success across the Atlantic. Nevertheless, the Bunnymen established during their brief tenure a name for themselves for their fun and fearless brand of music.

Pete De Freitas was born August 2, 1961, in Port of Spain, Trinidad, West Indies. Traveling to London in March of 1979, he found work as an echo. Actually, he replaced Echo, as the Bunnymen had affectionately named their electronic drum machine. Encouraged by their successful rehearsals and a record deal, the Bunnymen—lead singer Ian McCulloch, guitarist Will Sergeant, and bassist Les Pattinson—had decided to invest in a human drummer. Pete was the lucky winner and in May 1980 the group released a top-100 single—"Rescue" hit number sixty-two on the UK charts, and the group prepared for the release of their debut album. *Crocodiles* proved to be another hit,

reaching number seventeen on the British album chart. Although the following single, "The Puppet," did not find its way to the charts, the Bunnymen rebounded with their June 1981 album, *Heaven Up Here*, which inched into the number 100 spot in the UK and number 184 in the U.S. After a brief hiatus, the Bunnymen continued their upward trail with a number nineteen UK hit single, "The Back of Love."

Aiming for quality rather than quantity, Echo and the Bunnymen emerged from the studio in February of 1983 with their number eight hit, "The Cutter." This was followed by their first top-ten album—*Porcupine* reached the number two spot in Great Britain and ended up at number 137 in the U.S. The following year saw another top-ten British album when *Ocean Rain* reached number four in May. In a show of imagination, the Bunnymen organized an unprecedented event in support of their 1984 album. Calling the event "Echo and the Bunnymen Present a Crystal Day," the band led thousands of fans on a tour of Liverpool and ended the summer day with a live performance.

Echo and the Bunnymen continued their trend of success both in the studio and on the road. In February 1986, the lineup changed briefly when De Freitas was replaced by Mark Fox. By September of the same year, Pete had worked out his differences with the band and returned to the Bunnymen. The next two years were relatively quiet, but then the band returned to the charts with their remake of the Doors' "People Are Strange." The single, recorded for the soundtrack of the hit film *The Lost Boys*, reached number twenty-nine in the UK and would prove to be the group's last major hit.

In August of 1988, just five months after their return to the spotlight, the Bunnymen again began to drift apart. They denied the rumors that the band was dissolving for good, but the rumors gained ground when McCulloch announced his decision to commence a solo career. Nonetheless, the remaining Bunnymen stayed together, at least in name, until tragedy struck the following year.

On a warm June evening, Pete De Freitas decided to take his motorcycle out for a spin. He was in search of some fresh air and some time to contemplate any one of a hundred things. Whatever it was, he was not contemplating the road in front of him. Less than an hour later, Pete crashed his motorcycle into a car. He died instantly, and with him died Echo and the Bunnymen.

Dave Prater

Dave Prater, with his partner Sam Moore, provided the definition for soul in the 1960's. His life—and death—paralleled the emotional roller coaster of his music.

Dave Prater was born May 9, 1937, in Ocilla, Georgia, and his introduction to music came early, when he joined the church choir. The choir toured extensively, giving Prater an intensive musical background, but by the late fifties Dave began to lose interest in the gospel circuit. Although the gospel roots remained, his vocal style became more R&B influenced, and soon Dave embarked on a solo career. Dave started working throughout the South, playing small theaters and clubs where he frequently doubled as a cook. Prater's break came in 1958 at the King of Hearts club in Miami when Dave jumped onstage to join singer Sam Moore on "Doggin' Around." The audience loved it, and the two performers realized that they had something special. They decided to form a singing duo called Sam and Dave.

In 1960, the duo signed with the Roulette label, where they released several disappointing records over four years before switching to Stax/Atlantic. They started working with songwriters Isaac Hayes and David Porter and decided to use Booker T. and the MGs as well as the Memphis Horns for their Stax debut. Released in late 1965, "You Don't Know Like I Know" was a minor success, faring well on R&B charts. In June 1966, Sam and Dave used the same lineup for their second single, "Hold On, I'm Comin'," which became their first hit on the pop charts. Following their first major U.S. tour, the duo released three more top-ten R&B records, including "When Something Is Wrong With My Baby" and "You Got Me Hummin'." Although they constantly scored on the R&B charts, their pop success remained inconsistent. As Sam and Dave continued to tour, they earned the nickname "double dynamite" for their electrifying shows and passionate vocals.

The duo's winning elements came together in October 1967 with the release of "Soul Man." The single reached number two on the pop charts, went gold, and won Sam and Dave a Grammy. They struck it rich again a few months later with the follow-up hit, "I Thank You," and Sam and Dave were acknowledged to be the top soul duo of the sixties.

In 1968, the rosy scene darkened when Dave's personal life spiraled out of control. His marital difficulties culminated in May when he shot his wife during an argument, and though he was not prosecuted, the incident spread a pall over the duo's career. The two continued to record, but, try as they might, they could not regain their past glory. They came the closest in January of 1969 when "Soul Sister, Brown Sugar" climbed to number forty-one. The relationship between Sam and Dave dwindled as their success did, and in 1970 they decided to break up.

For the next decade, Sam and Dave pursued solo careers, reuniting now and again for short stints. In 1982, they parted ways for good when Dave recruited Sam Daniels. The two started to record and tour, under the familiar name of Sam and Dave. Not surprisingly, this move led to several lawsuits over the next four years.

Throughout their careers, the original Sam and Dave had indulged frequently in alcohol and various other drugs. By 1988 Sam had overcome his addiction, but Dave was not so lucky. In March of that year, Dave Prater was arrested in Patterson, New Jersey, for selling crack to an undercover cop. He was fined, sent to rehab, and put on probation for three years.

One month later, on April 9, a cleaned-up Dave went to visit his mother in Syracuse, Georgia. He was traveling down Interstate 5, at the age of fifty, when he lost control of his car, ran off the road, and slammed into a tree. Dave Prater was killed by the impact.

Chapter 7

.

Kamikazes

Kurt Cobain

In 1991, with the release of *Nevermind*, Nirvana single-handedly brought post-punk or "alternative" music into the mainstream of American rock 'n' roll. They combined the rock of every era and stripped the result down to its bare bones, creating an emotional, elemental sound that transformed the face of the music industry. Kurt Cobain's life and death embodied the Nirvana angst that captured the hearts and minds of millions of fans.

Kurt Cobain was born February 20, 1967, in Seattle. The child of divorced parents, Kurt turned to music at an early age and founded his first band, Fecal Matter, at the age of eighteen. Fecal Matter did not take off, and Kurt dabbled in several other bands before setting the first lineup for Nirvana: Kurt, Krist Novoselic, and Aaron Burckhard. The band began touring on the alternative circuit and developed a loyal following. Chad Channing and then Jason Everman replaced Burckhard, and the group debuted at the record stores in 1989 with *Bleach*. The supporting tour took Nirvana up and down the West Coast and across the Atlantic to kick off their first European tour in Newcastle, England, on October 10, 1989. After a few more singles and several personnel changes, the permanent lineup was set in 1990 when David Grohl came aboard as the drummer.

"Smells Like Teen Spirit" was performed for the first time on April 17, 1991, and thirteen days later the band signed a new record deal with Geffen Records. "Smells Like Teen Spirit" established Cobain's talent as a songwriter and performer, and with the backing of Geffen Records, Nirvana was unstoppable. They started recording *Nevermind* in May of 1991, and four months later released their groundbreaking offering. Returning from a successful European tour, Nirvana got right back on the road in support of their new album, with the opening show in Toronto. *Nevermind* debuted at number 144 on the charts and began its steady rise to the top. In constant motion, Nirvana returned from their worldwide Nevermind concert only to set off again, this time on a joint U.S. tour with Pearl Jam and the Red Hot Chili Peppers. They started 1992 with a blockbuster appearance on *Saturday Night Live* which shot *Nevermind* to number one on the charts.

In the midst of the 1992 European tour, Kurt took time off to marry Courtney Love in Waikiki, Hawaii, on February 24, 1992. Their child, Frances Bean Cobain, was born on August 18 of the same year, a month before Nirvana took two awards at the MTV music awards. Nirvana played their new single, "Lithium," to the appreciative MTV audience as an indication of the direction that Cobain was leading the band.

Nirvana's next album, *In Utero*, confirmed the intimations offered by "Lithium," characterized by Cobain's emotional pain and the raw, hard edge of the rhythm section. Soon after Nirvana emerged from the recording studio, they revealed their social conscience when they played a concert benefiting the victims of the Bosnian conflict. *In Utero* was released in the United States on September 21, 1993, and Nirvana began the In Utero tour the following month. After some video work, Nirvana continued their tour in Europe. The European tour was, however, destined to end in tragedy. The final show was played in Munich on February 29, 1994—leap year.

At the end of the strenuous tour, Kurt retreated to Rome to unwind. With the whirlwind over, Kurt had time to examine his life and he did not like what he saw. He tried to end it all on March 4, 1994, by overdosing on tranquilizers and champagne. Cobain arrived at the hospital in a coma, and the music world held its breath. This time, however, Kurt pulled through and he awoke the next day, requesting a milk shake as soon as he opened his eyes. Three days later, Kurt checked himself out of the hospital and returned to the States. It seemed that the near-death experience was a wake-up call for Cobain, and he confronted his pervasive heroin problem by checking into a rehab center in Marina Del Ray, California. Sources say that Kurt was becoming disenchanted with the greed and hypocrisy of the music business, and rumors flew about the fate of Nirvana.

Kurt Cobain left the rehab center on the evening of April 1, 1994. He had decided to withdraw from the planned Lollapalooza tour, and possibly from the business in general. It turned out that Cobain decided to withdraw completely, from life. On April 8, 1994, Kurt Cobain's body was found in the "greenhouse" above his garage at his Lake Washington house. He had shot himself in the head three days before and left a paradoxical suicide note that explained the love and hate that was Kurt Cobain:

> *To Boddah*
> *Speaking from the tongue of an experienced simpleton who obviously would rather be an emasculated, infantile complain-ee . . .*
>
> *I haven't felt the excitement of listening as well as creating music along with reading and*

writing for too many years now. I feel guilty beyond words about these things.

For example when we're backstage and the lights go out and the manic roar of the crowd begins, it doesn't affect me the way in which it did for Freddy Mercury, who seemed to love, relish in the love and adoration from the crowd, which is something I totally admire and envy. The fact is, I can't fool you, any one of you . . . The worst crime I can think of would be to rip people off by faking it and pretending as if I'm having 100% fun.

Sometimes I feel as if I should have a punch-in time clock before I walk out on stage. I've tried everything within my power to appreciate it (and I do, God, believe me I do, but it's not enough) . . . I must be one of those narcissists who only appreciate things when they're gone. I'm too sensitive. I need to be slightly numb to regain the enthusiasm I once had as a child.

There's good in all of us and I think I simply love people too much, so much that it makes me feel too fucking sad. The sad little, sensitive, unappreciative, Pisces, Jesus man!

I have a goddess of a wife who sweats ambition and empathy and a daughter who reminds me too much of what I used to be, full of love and joy, kissing everyone she meets because everyone is good and will do her no harm. And that terrifies me to the point where I can barely function. I can't stand the thought of Frances becoming the miserable, self-destructive, death rocker that I've become.

Thank you all from the pit of my burning, nauseous stomach for your letters and concern during the past years, I'm too much of an erratic, moody, baby! I don't have the passion anymore, and so remember, it's better to burn out than to fade away.

Peace, Love, Empathy.
Kurt Cobain

Frances and Courtney, I'll be at your altar. Please keep going, Courtney, for Frances. For her life, which will be so much happier without me.

I LOVE YOU, I LOVE YOU!

Courtney Love read excerpts of this haunting suicide note at the memorial service held in Seattle on April 10, 1994, and copies of the note raced around the world in magazines, books, and over the Internet. Thousands of fans were crushed and some, even in the face of all the evidence, refused to believe that Kurt would take his own life. Although many continue to worry the details of Kurt's life to this day, the world of rock 'n' roll is remaining faithful to Kurt's last words to his wife: it is remembering Cobain for the good that he created, and it will "keep going."

Ian Curtis

Like so many others, Ian Curtis is famous for what might have been rather than for what was. Joy Division was Ian's brainchild, a New Wave band with direction and an almost immediate following. With the loss of Ian, the band ceased to exist in its original form but gave birth to one of the major names in the rock of the eighties—New Order.

Ian Curtis grew up in Manchester, England, with a mild interest in music. When he and some of his friends happened into a local club in 1976 and heard the Sex Pistols do their thing, however, Ian's interest was transformed into an obsession. Ian and his three teenaged friends decided then and there to become a part of the musical movement they heard embodied in the Sex Pistols and the four formed a band. Undaunted by the fact that none of them played an instrument, they began to experiment with various instruments and sounds. Bernard Albrecht, Peter Hook, and Stephen Morris settled on their instruments, and Ian quickly emerged as the lead vocalist as well as the songwriter and inspirational leader.

Ian filled his voice to the brim with emotion and pain, and it was his raw, unique style which gained the band its identity. After two years of development, the band released its first single, "An Ideal for Living." The record earned them a recognized place in the industrial punk scene, but it also introduced the element that put Joy Division on the cutting edge of the New Wave movement. They had a denser, weightier, more solemn sound that would go down in history as one of the first appearances of the "gothic" style of New Wave.

The first release earned attention in the British New Wave circles, but the 1979 debut album *Unknown Pleasures* pulled Joy Division to the top. The group began touring Britain and Europe, and their success brought scores of record companies running. Joy Division decided to remain loyal to their original label, Factory Records. On the eve of what was to be a triumphant U.S. tour, the brass ring was snatched from Joy Division and replaced by grief and mourning. In May of 1980, Ian Curtis hanged himself.

Ian's reasons for his suicide are unclear. He left no note and his drastic measure left fans, friends, and band mates shocked and speechless. We can only speculate about his marital problems, clinical depression, and a worsening epileptic condition that drove him to take his own life. Joy Division was left in ruins with the departure of their leader. The U.S. tour was, of course, canceled, but the remaining trio began to book fall dates in order to fulfill contractual obligations. Gillian Gilbert, an experienced keyboardist and guitarist, came on board, and Bernard Albrecht changed his name to Sumner and took over the lead vocals. The band received plenty of attention from Curtis' suicide, but they floundered without their leader for two years. Ultimately, New Order emerged from the ashes, finding a new identity in the growing dance music world, and the inspiration of Ian Curtis lived on.

Terry Kath

The fact that Chicago drew such diverse audiences was a testament to the band's musical versatility. Their synthesis of rock, jazz, and R&B produced a sound that was no stranger to the charts. Although a mysterious accident took the life of Terry Kath, his vision has lived on.

Terry Allen Kath was born January 31, 1946, in Chicago, Illinois. Growing up in a musically oriented environment, Terry taught himself how to play several different instruments, including the guitar, bass, banjo, and drums. In the early sixties, he began playing bass in his first band, Jimmy and the Gentlemen, with school friend Walter Parazaider on sax. At DePaul University in 1966, Terry and Walter auditioned for a group called the Executives and met a drummer named Danny Seraphine. The three decided to form their own band, the Missing Links, and they recruited fellow students Robert Lamm on vocals and keyboards and Lee Loughnane on trumpet. After the audition of bassist Peter Cetera, Terry switched over to the guitar to complete the ensemble.

Now calling themselves the Big Thing, the band started to branch out, playing small club dates throughout the Midwest. They were discovered by Chicago musician James William Guercio, one of the hottest producers in the music industry. Guercio became their mentor, offering his business, management, and production skills on the condition that the band drop its current, Mafia-inspired name. The band agreed to the terms and made their debut as the Chicago Transit Authority on May 22, 1967, at the Stardust Lounge in Rockford, Illinois.

Under Guercio's guidance, the band relocated to Los Angeles, where Guercio paid their rent and enforced a strict rehearsal schedule. Pursuing an ambitious brand of rock fusion, the Chicago Transit Authority won immediate acclaim for the jazz/pop ballads featured on their debut album. This eponymous offering hit the stands in 1969 and remained on the charts for over three years.

In February of 1970, the band shortened its name to Chicago, following threats from Chicago mayor Richard Daley. Their second album was another self-titled hit that made number four and stayed on the charts for 134 weeks. The record promotion opened with two weeks in Europe, followed by an eleven-month U.S. tour. The single

"Make Me Smile" made number nine, leading off a very impressive string of hits including "Does Anybody Really Know What Time It Is," "Beginnings/Color My World," "Saturday in the Park," "Just You 'n' Me," "Old Days," and the number-one "If You Leave Me Now." Chicago also hit the album charts with *25 or 6 to 4*. With Terry, Robert, and Peter sharing lead vocals and the addition of trombonist James Pankow and percussionist Laudir de Oliveira, Chicago evolved into a supergroup enjoying international renown.

On January 23, 1978, Terry and his wife attended a party at the home of a friend in Woodland Hills, California. After a day of drinking and socializing, the party was just breaking up when Terry removed a gun from his pocket and started twirling it. When roadie Don Johnson asked him to stop he replied, "Don't worry, it's not loaded. See?" With alcohol-induced confidence, Terry Kath put the gun to his head, pulled the trigger, and died in front of the remaining partygoers, at the age of thirty-one. Although the strange circumstances sparked a murder/suicide controversy, the ensuing investigation proved nothing.

Once the shock of the tragedy wore off, Chicago decided to continue. Singer/guitarist Donnie Dacus was chosen as Terry's replacement, and the band remained successful well into the eighties. Terry Kath is buried at Forest Lawn, 1712 S. Glendale, Glendale, California.

Richard Manuel

The Band steered rock 'n' roll in a simpler direction, standing out against the frivolity and extravagance of the psychedelics. These Canadians made their way through the world of folk by foregoing the hippie image and focusing on making melodious music. The Band preferred jeans and suit coats to beads and sparkles, and their most important props were their guitars.

When The Band began in Canada in 1960, they called themselves the Hawks, after lead singer Ronnie Hawkins. Three years later, they split from Hawkins and renamed themselves the Levon Helm Sextet and later Levon and the Hawks. The members of The Band were: lead singer and drummer Levon Helm, Robbie Robertson on vocals and guitar, Garth Hudson on the grand organ, pianist Richard Manuel, bassist Rick Danko, Harvey Brooks on bass, Al Kooper on keyboards, vocalist Bruce Bruno, and Jerry Penfound on sax. Bruno and Penfound left in 1964, and in 1965 the still sizable group recorded a single, "The Stones I Throw," under the Atco label. Although the album did not take off on the charts, it found its way into the hands of Albert Grossman, manager of Bob Dylan. Grossman liked what he heard and decided that he had found the band to back Dylan on his tour of the UK. They traveled throughout Britain, did several shows in the U.S., and returned to Britain in 1966.

The Band was with Dylan in the early days of his monumental switch from the acoustic sound to the electric. The transition was less than popular with the core of Dylan's folk fans, and Dylan and The Band often were forced to play over the boos of the audience. The fans claimed that they had been betrayed by their champion, but Dylan and The Band refused to turn back. The persistence paid off and by the time the seventies rolled around, Dylan and The Band was playing over standing ovations instead of boos.

Between tours with Dylan, The Band began to make a name for itself in the recording studio. The first album was born at Big Pink, the name given to the old farmhouse near Woodstock, New

York, where the group rehearsed. The album, *Music from Big Pink*, came out in 1968 and represented their signature fusion of R&B and country-western. The album contained several Dylan compositions but also some bold new originals that exhibited The Band's versatility and creativity. "The Weight," one of the top singles on the album, embodied the group's sound and was covered by many artists including Aretha Franklin, the Supremes, and the Temptations. The song also came out in 1969 on the *Easy Rider* soundtrack.

Encouraged by their debut success, The Band returned to the recording studio and in 1969 released an eponymous album which rose to the number nine spot on the charts. The Band embarked on their first independent tour later in the year, with their first stop at the Winterland Ballroom in San Francisco. The tour got off to a slow start when Robertson declared that he was suffering from too much stage fright to go on. In a panic, the group summoned a hypnotist who put Robertson under so the show could go on. The Band went on to a successful tour and the incident inspired their next album, *Stage Fright*, which went to number five on the charts and produced a hit single of the same name.

The Band spent the first half of the 1970's turning out successful albums and spent a good part of their time on the top-forty album chart. *Cahoots* hit number twenty-one in 1971 and *Rock of Ages* shot up to number six the following year. In 1974, The Band found themselves backing up Bob Dylan on his albums *Before the Flood* and Dylan's *Planet Waves*. On their own again in 1975, The Band released the number twenty-eight hit *Moondog Matinee* and came out the next year with *Northern Lights–Southern Cross*, which rose to number twenty-five.

After their string of hits, The Band decided that it was time to withdraw from the scene, but they decided to go out with a bang. They returned to the Winterland, their touring birthplace, for their swan song performance on November 25, 1976, and they invited all of the shining lights in the rock 'n' roll sky to perform with them. The all-star cast included Bob Dylan, Ringo Starr, Neil Young, Joni Mitchell, Van Morrison, Paul Butterfield, Muddy Waters, Ronnie Hawkins, Ron Wood, Emmylou Harris, Neil Diamond, and Dr. John. Each guest came on stage for one song with The Band and the event was a raging success. Bill Graham, the manager of The Band, tended to every detail, and the result was a complete victory—Graham even arranged a full-scale Thanksgiving dinner for the entire audience.

The Band split apart after their triumphant finale, and the members attempted various solo and film careers, with limited success. After a decade as individuals, The Band reunited (minus Robertson) in 1986 for a tour of the U.S. Although the tour was a profitable experience, The Band could not return to their former glory, and the decline was too much for one member to take. On March 6, 1986, the tour ended, and The Band as it was ceased to exist, when Richard Manuel hanged himself after a show in Winter Park, Florida. Manuel could not take the distance they had slipped from Winterland to Winter Park, and he bowed out of life.

The Band as a whole did not give up so easily, and in 1990 they reunited for Roger Waters' concert of *The Wall* at the Berlin Wall. In the process, they garnered a four-record deal with Columbia and The Band played on.

Del Shannon

Del Shannon is perhaps best known for his runaway hit "Runaway." Although he charted several other singles and albums, Del was never satisfied with his success. Sadly, Del Shannon's life and death exemplified the curse of rock 'n' roll fame.

Charles Westover was born on December 30, 1939, in the small midwestern town of Coopersville, Michigan. At the age of fourteen, Charles began listening to country and western music, and Hank Williams soon became an idol. Young Westover took up the guitar, practicing in the woods to avoid his father's disapproval, and soon he began to perform in school shows. After graduating from high school, Charles married sweetheart Shirley Nash and enlisted in the army a year later. While stationed in Germany, Charles hosted the "Get Up and Go" radio show on the Armed Forces Network. Charles got a hardship discharge in 1958 when his father had a stroke, and he returned home with dreams of stardom.

In 1960, Charles moved to Battle Creek, Mississippi, and changed his name to Del Shannon. He sold carpet by day and played with the Charley Johnson Show Band at the Hi-Lo Club by night. The band caught the attention of a well-known local DJ and a management/production team who led them to Detroit's Big Top label. The Charley Johnson Show Band made demos of several songs before their debut recording session at Bell Sound in New York, on January 21, 1961.

In early 1961, Del made a major conquest with his solo record premiere, "Runaway" (cowritten with keyboardist Max Crook), which reached the top of the charts in twenty-one countries. The song sold over a million copies after four weeks at number one, giving Del Shannon what would prove to be his only gold record. "Runaway" also inspired over 200 cover versions, including one by Elvis Presley.

With "Runaway" under his belt, Del was on top of the world and soon followed it up with several more hits, including "Hats Off to Larry," which reached number six. Soon Del embarked on a smash world tour, with his London show featuring the Beatles as an opening act. In 1963, Del covered the Beatles song, "From Me to You," introducing the Beatles sound to the U.S. before the Beatles themselves had crossed the Atlantic. Later that year, Del Shannon was voted "most popular male singer" in England, and in November he started his own record label, Bar-Lee.

In spite of the outward success, or perhaps because of it, Del was increasingly plagued by depression and self-doubt. He became embroiled in a lawsuit with his managers and he began to drink excessively. Still, Del continued to work, and after a three-year dry spell he returned to the charts in January 1965 with "Keep Searchin' (We'll Follow the Sun)." This song proved to be his last recording success for over seventeen years, but he did find a new niche—as a songwriter. After penning several hits, Del transformed himself again in 1969 when he entered the world of production. His biggest production success was "Gypsy Woman" for old friend Brian Hyland—the song reached number three in 1970.

In 1970, Del resumed his singing career, recording and touring primarily in Britain. Del found, however, that no one was interested in his new material. His concerts were basically "oldies" shows, and the stagnation depressed him. He left the music industry in 1972 and entered the real estate business, but he found no joy in his monetary success. Shannon's alcoholism worsened, until in 1978 his wife threatened to leave him and he checked into rehab.

Now that he was sober, Del finally made a return to the top forty in February 1982 when "Sea of Love" reached number thirty-three on the charts in February of 1982. The musical rebirth was not mirrored by a personal rehabilitation, however, and his marriage finally cracked under the pressure of the years of alcohol abuse. By the mid-eighties, it was over. Del pulled through this personal setback and continued to make music, recording, touring, and offering his old favorites to television and film. Rumored to be the top choice to replace Roy Orbison in the Traveling Wilburys, Del was on the verge of a major comeback, but it seemed that ultimate success was fated to elude him.

In the midst of the public success, Del's private life again began to suffer. His second marriage was on the brink of falling apart, and both of his families were experiencing financial difficulties. In 1990, Del became severely depressed and began taking Prozac. The years of disappointment, of balancing on the edge of superstardom, came to a head when the Rock 'N' Roll Hall of Fame asked Del to present an award after years of ignoring his own achievements. It was February 8, 1990, when Del Shannon decided to end the private struggles and the public disappointments. On that date, Del walked into the studio of his Santa Clarita home, sat down, put a .22 caliber rifle to his head and pulled the trigger.

Chapter 8

.

Slow Fade

Tom Fogerty

Like many of the hippie bands, Creedence Clearwater Revival was based in San Francisco. But unlike many of the other San Francisco bands, Creedence Clearwater represented a reaction against the excesses of the psychedelic era and a return to the basics of rock 'n' roll. The group's unique blend of rockabilly harmonies and southern groove was known as "swamp rock." The simplicity of swamp rock was a refreshing change after the sensory overload provided by masters like Jimi Hendrix and Cream.

Tom Fogerty was born in Berkeley, California, on November 9, 1941. He and his brother John were raised in the Bay Area and began to play guitar at a very young age. In 1963 they formed a band known as Tommy Fogerty and the Blue Velvets and began to perform at school dances and other local venues. The Fogerty brothers were joined by Stu Cook on bass and Doug "Cosmos" Clifford on drums, and the group, now called Vi-

sion, went on the quest for a record contract. They signed with Fantasy Records and, at the suggestion of their manager Hy Weiss, changed the name again to the Golliwogs. Weiss thought that Golliwogs sounded British and that it would help the band capitalize on the popularity of the British Invasion.

The Golliwogs released their debut single, "Don't Tell Me No Lies," in November of 1964, but the record enjoyed little success. The subsequent releases proved equally mediocre and the group temporarily disbanded in 1966 when John Fogerty and Doug Clifford were drafted into the army. When the two GIs returned the following year, the band reassembled under the name Creedence Clearwater Revival. "Creedence" was the name of a beloved friend, "Clearwater" was reminiscent of a popular beer commercial, and "Revival" described what they hoped to do. They did indeed come back to life, and when they released their first single, "Suzie Q," they finally broke into the charts. "Suzie Q" went to number eleven and the self-titled album that followed rose to number fifty-two and stayed on the charts for seventeen months.

Creedence Clearwater Revival had found their niche in the music industry, and their successes continued. In 1969, they reached the number two spot with "Proud Mary," an innovative composition laced with Cajun nuances. "Proud Mary" told the story of life on the Mississippi and was covered by countless artists, including Elvis Presley and Ike and Tina Turner. In 1969 the band released two more hits, "Bad Moon Rising" and "Green River," both of which reached number two on the charts. In 1970, a pronounced R&B influence began to appear in their work, and this new direction proved equally lucrative. "Down on the Corner," "Fortunate Son," "Travelin' Band," "Who'll Stop the Rain," and "Up Around the Bend" all sat in the top twenty in 1970. In 1971 the hits were "Have You Ever Seen the Rain" and "Sweet Hitch-Hiker." During their reign on the singles charts, Creedence Clearwater also enjoyed considerable success on the album charts. *Bayou Country*, *Green River*, *Willy and the Poor Boys*, and *Cosmo's Factory* all spent some time on the top-ten album chart in 1969 and 1970.

Always popular performers, Creedence Clearwater Revival was a favorite at the festivals of the late sixties. In 1970 they embarked on a highly successful European tour. During the tour, however, dissent brewed among the quartet when Cook and Clifford decided that John Fogerty had been dominating the songwriting and artistic direction of the group for too long. Discouraged by the unrest and perhaps feeling overshadowed himself, Tom Fogerty left the band in 1971 to pursue a solo career. Tom left with a flourish, for his last album with Creedence Clearwater Revival, *Pendulum*, reached number five on the charts.

John Fogerty yielded to his band mates' complaints and turned over the control of the next album to Cook and Clifford. The May 1972 release of *Mardi Gras* made it clear that there was a reason that John had led the group for so many years. The album was a failure with the public and the critics, and it soon became known as "Fogerty's Revenge." After Creedence Clearwater Revival folded, John Fogerty eventually went on to a successful solo career, with his 1985 album *Centerfield* topping the charts.

Brother Tom did not fare as well. His solo debut was released the month after the *Mardi Gras* debacle hit the stores, with equivalent results. Tom continued to record, with minimal success. On September 6, 1990, two decades after his ride at the top of the music world, Tom Fogerty died in Arizona of respiratory failure. He was forty-nine years old.

Alan Freed

As a renowned DJ, Alan Freed made many contributions to the world of rock 'n' roll—not the least of which was its name. His Moon Dog Ball and other concerts helped to create the "rock 'n' roll" youth culture that persists today.

Aldon James Freed was born on December 15, 1922, in Johnstown, Pennsylvania, and grew up in Salem, Ohio. As a teenager, Alan played the trombone and fronted a jazz band, the Sultans of Swing, before joining the U.S. Army. After an honorable discharge, Freed earned a masters degree in engineering from Ohio State and then turned his attention to radio. Alan was a sportscaster, a program director, and a disc jockey, bouncing from station to station in Ohio and Pennsylvania. His rise to fame started at WJW in Cleveland in 1951. Even though he was white, Alan became a top rhythm and blues disc jockey and built a major reputation among black audiences. Adopting the pseudonym "Moon Dog," he caught the spirit of the music, often singing along, and his reputation spread as his popular show was syndicated in other midwestern cities.

Alan Freed not only brought new music to the masses—he brought a new name to the music. The words "rock" and "roll" often denoted sexual content in R&B lyrics, and Alan thought that putting them together described the rhythms and riffs of the music he was playing. The new classification "rock and roll" caught on quickly. It was hip and stations liked using the phrase as a cautious way to ease the new music into the mainstream while avoiding any racial stigma. It worked; the term and the music quickly entered the mainstream of teenage culture.

Alan was an opportunist and it wasn't long before he realized the immensity of the market he had tapped into. He promoted the Moon Dog Ball, an integrated concert bill that drew a crowd of over 25,000 to the Cleveland Arena; the arena's official capacity was less than half that. Local officials pulled the plug halfway through the show, sending mobs of kids rampaging though the streets. It was the first rock 'n' roll riot.

Alan's activities did not escape the attention of the music industry chiefs on the East Coast. In 1954, WINS in New York hired him for the then enormous sum of $75,000 a year, a gamble which showed immediate dividends as the station's ratings shot through the roof. Alan soon began staging live shows, establishing box office records at the Paramount Theater in Brooklyn. He was also credited with cowriting several rock standards, most notably Chuck Berry's "Maybellene" and the Moonglows' "Sincerely." He appeared in a handful of early rock 'n' roll movies, including *Rock Around the Clock*. By 1957, Alan had inspired over 4,000 fan clubs.

The year 1958, however, marked the beginning of a tumultuous fall from grace for Alan Freed. He was charged with inciting a riot after a stabbing and several beatings took place at one of his Boston concerts. The charge was dropped a year and a half later, but rock 'n' roll shows were subsequently banned in several cities and Alan was kicked out of the concert business. He jumped WINS for New York's WABC but was quickly fired for refusing to sign an affidavit that said he had never accepted payola (kickback for giving an album airtime). He was then indicted in 1960 and three years later pleaded guilty to taking $2,700 from two record companies. He escaped with only a fine and suspended sentence. Ostracized, Alan's last radio job was a brief stint at KDAY in Los Angeles.

Broke and under indictment for tax evasion, Alan died in obscurity of uremic poisoning in Palm Springs on January 20, 1965. He is buried at Fancliff Cemetery in Hartsdale, New York.

Muddy Waters

Muddy Waters, the father of Chicago Blues, was an inspiration for countless blues, R&B, and rock musicians spanning several generations.

He brought the blues sound to the white world, awing young musicians like the Rolling Stones, Eric Clapton, and Bob Dylan. In fact, the Stones actually named themselves after the title of one of Muddy Waters' hits, "Rollin' Stone." Throughout his career, Waters experimented with various approaches and idioms while maintaining the integrity of the blues sound. His was an electric version of Delta country blues, and when he electrified his sound, he electrified audiences all over the world.

McKinley Morganfield was born in 1915 in Rolling Fork, Mississippi. His mother died when he was three years old, and McKinley was raised by his grandmother in Clarksdale, Mississippi. Growing up in the country, McKinley developed an affinity for mud puddles which earned him the nickname that would take him to the top. He played the harmonica and the guitar as a young boy, and at the age of seventeen Muddy Waters began to perform at local parties. His idols were two blues greats, Son House and Robert Johnson. He combined House's rich solid tones with Johnson's playfulness and agility, as well as a creativity and vision that were all his own.

After a brief foray into the St. Louis music scene, Waters returned to Mississippi and opened a juke house, a place of whiskey, poker, and live music furnished by the owner himself. Word of his music traveled far, and in the summer of 1941 a representative from the Library of Congress showed up to record the music of the Mississippi Delta. Muddy Waters told *Rolling Stone* magazine:

He brought his stuff down and recorded me right in my house and when he played back the first song I sounded just like anybody's records. Man, you don't know how I felt that Saturday afternoon when I heard that voice and it was my own voice. Later on he sent me two copies of the pressing and a check for twenty bucks, and I carried that record up to the corner and put it on the jukebox. Just played it and played it and said, "I can do it, I can do it."

Muddy Waters had another session with Alan Lomax from the Library of Congress in July of 1942, and both sessions ended up on the Testament release *Down on Stovall's Plantation*.

After hearing his own potential, Muddy Waters decided to try his fortune in Chicago, the blues capital of the north. He moved in with his uncle and took two day jobs while trying to break into the scene by night. Big Bill Broonzy was the king of the blues when Waters arrived, and Muddy got his big break when he became the opening act for Broonzy at some of his club gigs. It was during this stint that Muddy Waters received a gift that would be a ticket to success: his uncle gave him an electric guitar.

Armed with his electric guitar, Muddy Waters began to record his work. His first offerings, recorded under the Columbia label in 1946, were never released. He switched over to the Aristocrat label, and after a few more unsuccessful sessions, he released two singles, "I Can't Be Satisfied" and "I Feel Like Going Home." With these recording successes, Muddy Waters began to draw huge crowds at his nightclub performances. His popularity continued to grow, and later in 1948 Waters released "Rollin' Stone" under the newly named Chess label (previously Aristocrat). "Rollin' Stone" smashed the R&B charts and attracted widespread acclaim. The song was assured a place in history when the band that would become a giant of rock 'n' roll decided to name themselves after its title.

By 1950, Muddy Waters had assembled a truly impressive lineup in his band: Little Walter on harp, Jimmy Rogers on guitar, Elgin Evans on drums, Otis Spann on piano, Big Crawford on bass, and Muddy Waters as lead vocalist and slide guitarist. This group churned out a string of hits, including "Hoochie Coochie Man," which went to number eight on the R&B chart; "I Just Want to Make Love to You," which hit number four, and "I'm Ready." These were high-profile, hard-edged compositions by songwriter Willie Dixon, perhaps heavier than Muddy's own style. They attracted attention, however, and helped to propel him into the national and international spotlight. The hard edge stayed, and the high energy band, now known as the Headhunters, gave performance after commanding performance. Muddy Waters' vocal style became increasingly aggressive to match the heavy rhythms of his supporting musicians.

As the fifties progressed, the members of the Headhunters began individually to seek fame in their own right as solo performers. The band dissolved by 1956 and an era of Muddy Waters' career came to a close.

In 1958, Muddy Waters crossed the Atlantic to pursue his career in the United Kingdom. His electric blues found enthusiastic audiences and eager musical followers. American blues and R&B were the newest British craze, and Muddy Waters embodied the sound. He returned to the U.S. in 1960 for the Newport Folk Festival and found that the mainstream of his own countrymen were beginning to appreciate the Delta Blues. Muddy Waters' personal feelings of triumph were diminished, however, when he saw that his music, celebrated by the white community, was being virtually ignored by blacks. It was a phenomenon that would plague Muddy Waters throughout his life.

After his success at the Folk Festival, Muddy Waters retreated into the shadows for over a decade, releasing no major records. Then in 1972, he was booked to record *The London Muddy Waters Sessions* with an all-star cast of Rory Gallagher, Steve Winwood, Rick Grech, and Mitch Mitchell. In spite of his respect for their talents, Muddy was not pleased with the outcome of the sessions. He did not feel that the four rockers were able to produce his specific sound. His sound was subtle and nuanced, with endless variations that made it difficult to follow. Muddy told *Rolling Stone*:

When I plays on stage with my band, I have to get in there with my guitar and try to bring the sound down to me. But no sooner than I quit playing, it goes back to another different sound. My blues look so simple, so easy to do, but it's not. They say my blues is the hardest blues in the world to play.

Muddy found someone who could play his kind of blues in guitarist Johnny Winter, and in 1976 Muddy Waters had signed on to the Blue Sky label with Winter. The duo recorded *Hard Again* in two days, and the album represented a return both to the spotlight and to Muddy's original Chicago blues sound. The album scored a Grammy for the blues master and a rousingly successful tour followed. *I'm Ready* proved that the comeback success was not a fluke, and the next album, *Muddy "Mississippi" Waters Live*, wreaked equal havoc on the charts. The year 1980 saw the release of *King Bee*, an appropriate title for the recrowned king of the blues.

Muddy Waters left this world in 1983, not in any showstopping performance, but rather by slipping away in his sleep. The hordes at his funeral were a testament to his supreme contributions to the art of the blues. Another testament came two years later when the city of Chicago changed the name of 43rd Street to Muddy Waters Drive. Blues musicians, R&B musicians, rock musicians—artists from all genres would join together in acknowledging Muddy Waters as one of the true originals, a wellspring of inspiration and a master.

Chapter 9

.

Odd Outtakes

Brian Jones

The Rolling Stones have been called the "world's greatest rock and roll band," and there is no doubt that with the emergence of Britain's band of bad boys, the rock world was changed forever. They embodied the free spirit of their music, with fast lifestyles and rebellious attitudes. The Rolling Stones proved that a white band could play the blues, or their version of the blues, and Brian Jones' guitar blazed the trail.

Brian Jones was born Lewis Brian Hopkin-Jones in Cheltenham Gloucester, England, on February 28, 1942. Jones grew up with a love of music, especially of the American blues, and in the early sixties he became active in the R&B scene in London, joining Alexis Korner's Blues Incorporated. In 1962, two new members were initiated into the Blues Incorporated; their names were Mick Jagger and Keith Richards. The trio soon took control of the band, and in 1963 Jones recruited Charlie Watts on drums, Ian Stewart on keyboards, and Bill Wyman on bass. Jones named the group after the title of a Muddy Waters song, "Rollin' Stone."

The band's big break came when they were hired as the house band of the Crawdaddy Club in London. It was there that Andrew Loog Oldham and Eric Easton spotted them in April of 1963 and offered their services as managers. The group accepted the offer, and Oldham and Easton began to work their magic. The pair had decided that the key to matching the Beatles' overwhelming success, especially in the lucrative American market, was through opposition. The Rolling Stones would be the dark side of the boyish, clean-cut image of the Beatles. The naughty British band would contrast starkly and, Oldham hoped, favorably with the nice. The commitment to the new look ran so deep that in that first year Ian Stewart was dropped from the group because he looked too "good." He did, however, remain involved with the band, playing on some studio recordings and managing the group on the road.

The Rolling Stones signed on with Impact for their first record deal, but their contract was leased out to Decca Records (the label that had recently rejected the Beatles). Their debut single was a remake of Chuck Berry's "Come On," released on June 7, 1963, and it reached number twenty-one on the British charts. They climbed the charts still higher with the subsequent release of a Lennon/McCartney single, "I Wanna Be Your Man," which reached number twelve. Their debut eponymous album, released in May of the next year, topped the UK album charts and almost broke into the U.S. top ten, hitting number eleven. A single featured on the album, Buddy Holly's "Not Fade Away," did find a place in the top ten singles chart in the U.S., peaking at number three.

With their chart successes in the United States, the Rolling Stones embarked on an American tour in June of 1964. The reception was mixed, and the band realized that they could never enter the upper echelons of rock performers until they started to play original material. Knowing that covers would never lead them to superstardom, Jagger and Richards began their songwriting careers. Their efforts paid off. "The Last Time" hit number nine on the U.S. charts, and with the release of "Satisfaction" in 1965 the Rolling Stones achieved the coveted number one spot on the U.S. singles chart. "Get Off of My Cloud" and "19th Nervous Breakdown" also enjoyed considerable success on both sides of the Atlantic.

During these years, Brian Jones enjoyed personal artistic growth. He experimented with other instruments, playing the keyboards, the cello, and the recorder in the 1967 recording of the number one hit, "Ruby Tuesday." Jones may have, nonetheless, been dissatisfied with the leading creative roles assumed by Jagger and Richards as songwriters. It seems that Jones was jealous of their position, and he often retaliated by posing as the group's leader in interviews and other public appearances. In 1967, many of these interviews were focused on something other than the music, as Jagger, Richards, and Jones were all three arrested on the charge of drug possession. They were the first rockers to achieve this dubious honor, and the resulting court proceedings did much to confirm the bad boy image of the Stones.

That same year brought the release of a new album, *Their Satanic Majesties Request*, and the title of the record may have done as much for the Rolling Stones' image as the trials. The album featured a new psychedelic sound with a hard edge, and Richards began to experiment with the jagged guitar lines that would become his signature. *Their Satanic Majesties Request* uncovered some disputes that Brian Jones felt with the rest of the group over the musical direction that the band was taking. Oldham likewise began to lose touch with the group's vision, and after the release of the album he was sacked. The harder sound continued with the hit single "Jumpin' Jack Flash" released in 1968 as well as in the album *Beggars Banquet* of the same year. The songs from this album, especially "Street Fighting Man," represented the Stones at their greatest and most mature. "Sympathy for the Devil," another track on the album, was reflective perhaps of the rough edge that had entered their lifestyles as well as their music. Sympathy with Satan would take its toll, and Brian Jones was to be the victim.

Brian Jones, as much as Mick Jagger, was addicted to fame. Brian had been responsible in many ways for the founding of the group. He had named the Rolling Stones. He had conceived of many of their preening stage personas. Musically, however, Jones added more texture than innovation, branching out into other instruments and sounds but not really providing any visionary direction. As the sixties wore on, perhaps in response to his frustration at his backseat in the creative process and in media attention, Jones turned to drugs and alcohol. A rift developed in the band, with Jagger and Richards on one side and Jones on the other. Jones became increasingly ineffective, with the poisons he took robbing him of musical reliability. After his minimal contributions to *Beggars Banquet*, Jones was asked to leave the group.

A month after Brian Jones left the Rolling Stones, he departed from the land of the living. At his country house on the evening of July 3, 1969, Jones loaded himself with alcohol and barbiturates and was found the next morning drowned in the swimming pool. There were rumors of suicide. There were rumors of foul play, perhaps perpetrated by fellow Stones. These rumors were nowhere to be found, however, at the memorial service two days later in Hyde Park when Jagger read from Shelley and released a thousand butterflies in Brian's honor.

Keith Relf

The Yardbirds were the first of many British groups to look to the R&B masters of the United States for their primary inspiration. They were the first, in fact, to combine the rock sound with an ethnic, nonrock overtone which resulted in an important step in the evolution of rock and roll. The Yardbirds' most notable contribution was perhaps their innovative use of the guitar riff and feedback, a technique that would feed the psychedelic bands, progressive rock, and heavy metal, and provide particular inspiration for Led Zeppelin. Keith Relf was the voice of the Yardbirds and a constant in the midst of perpetual lineup changes. He was accompanied by such guitar greats as Eric Clapton, Jimmy Page, and Jeff Beck during his tenure with the Yardbirds, before embarking on a solo career.

Keith Relf was born on March 22, 1943, in Richmond, London. At an early age, Relf was exposed to the London music scene, and he quickly became an active participant. In 1963, he joined up with Paul Samwell-Smith on bass, Chris Dreja on rhythm guitar, and Anthony "Top" Topham on guitar to form the Metropolitan Blues Quartet. After slipping a few gigs under their belt, the group entered the R&B circuit in London and changed their name to the Yardbirds. Soon after their name change, Giorgio Gomelsky noticed them and hired them as the house band in his Crawdaddy Club—the previous house band at the Crawdaddy Club had been the Rolling Stones. During the Crawdaddy Club era, Topham quit the band and was replaced by none other than Eric Clapton.

Giorgio Gomelsky booked the new lineup on a tour of the United Kingdom, backing up Sonny Boy Williamson. The debut album in 1964, *Five Live Yardbirds*, was received with mild interest, but its impact was long-range, for it was indirectly responsible for one of the Yardbird's greatest hits. Songwriter Graham Gouldman heard the album

and offered the group a song that he had written. This single, "For Your Love," gained the Yardbirds entry into the top ten, hitting number six on the U.S. charts. The commercial success was a mixed blessing, however, because guitarist Eric Clapton became dissatisfied with the artistic direction that "For Your Love" implied for the group. The Yardbirds found a replacement on short notice, and Jeff Beck was welcomed into the group. He was a perfect fit, his technicality and creativity complementing the group's vision.

Keith Relf played a major role in the conception and execution of the next hit single, "Heart Full of Soul." With the help of Paul Samwell-Smith, Relf introduced a new influence into their rock sound, namely the haunting melodies and undulations of the music of India. Relf brought in a sitarist to create the sound he wanted for the new song, but the effect was not what Keith was looking for. He found it instead within the group; Beck would simulate the sound of the sitar on his guitar, using his technical skill to achieve the subtleties. The result was a success, and "Heart Full of Soul" reached number two in the United Kingdom and hit the number six spot on the American charts.

The next album, *Having A Rave-Up With the Yardbirds*, represented a combination of much that had gone before, a fusion of the old and the new. The old came on side two, which featured Eric Clapton on previously recorded tracks from *Five Live Yardbirds*. Side one was a synthesis of many of the new influences that the Yardbirds had been exploring in the last year or two. The Indian overtones were present in some of the tracks, and a Gregorian chant provided the foundation of the hit, "Still I'm Sad." Another new development was the growing emphasis on Samwell-Smith's bass line, giving the songs a weight and driving quality.

The Yardbirds were entering a new phase in their music, one that many would say presaged the genre of heavy metal. The hit single, "Train Kept a Rollin', I'm a Man," epitomized the fusion of the now traditional use of R&B with the new and innovative guitar rifts and the commanding presence of the bass line. The link to heavy metal would prove tangible when in 1966 Jeff Beck dropped out and was replaced by Jimmy Page. Jimmy Page continued the trend toward a rougher sound, and the group continued to evolve in spite of numerous dropouts and replacements. Throughout all of the turmoil, however, Keith Relf stood as a steady influence and leader, combining the founding vision of the Yardbirds with the creative growth to which they all aspired.

Although several more successful singles followed, by the middle of 1968 it was clear that the group had been technically overtaken. Jimi Hendrix and Eric Clapton had access to a level of virtuosity with which the Yardbirds could simply not compete. The creative vision of Relf and his band mates was not matched by the level of skill that the emerging masters exhibited, and in July of 1968 the Yardbirds disbanded.

The Yardbirds was a stepping-stone not only in the evolution of rock, but also for several of the group's individual members. Eric Clapton catapulted to the top after parting ways with the Yardbirds. Jimmy Page went on to found the legendary Led Zeppelin. What then of Keith Relf, the Yardbirds' cofounder and steady guiding light? For him, the Yardbirds was the summit rather than a point on an upward trajectory. He certainly did not leave the music world after the group parted ways. He continued to record, both as a solo act and with a variety of bands. He founded Renaissance, but unfortunately the group's name did not reflect the reality of Relf's career. His personal life fared better than his professional life, and in 1968, the year that the band ceased to exist, Relf's son was born. Relf eventually tried to combine family with music and in 1975 he decided to form a band with his sister. They began developing songs and rehearsing, often in Relf's London home.

It was during one of these homegrown rehearsal sessions that Relf's life was cut tragically short. After an encouraging jam with his sister, Keith was fiddling around with his electric guitar. His eight-year-old son entered the room. The currents of electricity that had helped Keith Relf make music for twenty years suddenly turned against him, and Keith Relf was electrocuted at the age of thirty-three. Relf's body was found holding the live electric guitar, with his small son looking on in terror.

Keith Relf was a major contributor to the world of rock 'n' roll, one perhaps who was never rewarded commensurate to his offerings. He lived for several years at the top of the charts without sacrificing creative exploration. Commercial success did not stymie the musical growth of the Yardbirds as it did many other groups. The group ran its course in the river of rock development, and when the time came, the group gracefully with-

drew. Relf faded with the group, and died in relative obscurity. His lack of notoriety is not an indication, however, of an unworthy musician. It is rather a reflection of the natural progression of artistic expression and of the often cruel hand of fate.

Dennis Wilson

The Beach Boys, the golden boys of rock 'n' roll, sang about the lighter side of life—teenage love, California style. Their "surf rock" defined the myth of the West Coast, and they embodied the youth and exuberance that went along with the myth. Their early music, especially, was clean and energetic, though later they began to explore the darker side of love. Throughout their career, the Beach Boys' music was characterized by complex, overlapping harmonies. Their sound had far-ranging influence, even inspiring Paul McCartney in his work on *Sgt. Pepper's Lonely Hearts Club Band*. The case of Dennis Wilson is the story of a mediocre drummer surfing the waves of rock 'n' roll fame.

The Beach Boys grew up together, for the band consisted of three brothers, their cousin, and a neighbor. Brian Wilson, as bassist and songwriter, led the group's musical development. Brother Carl Wilson and neighbor Al Jardine played the guitar. Cousin Mike Love crooned Brian's songs. Dennis Wilson, born December 4, 1944, in Inglewood, California, kept the rhythm with his drums. The Wilsons, Love, and Jardine came together in 1961 and formed a band called first Carl and the Passions, then Kenny and the Cadets, next the Pendletons, before finally arriving at the Beach Boys. Murry Wilson became the group's manager, and Dad signed the Beach Boys first with the local X Label. The band recorded

"Surfin' " for their debut single, but the song was virtually ignored by the public. Discouraged by the failure, Jardine quit soon after the release and was replaced by David Marks.

It turned out that Jardine left just a little too soon, for in 1962 "Surfin' " was sold to the Candix Label and hit the Top 100, reaching number seventy-five in the U.S. When Candix folded, months later, Murry took the band to Capitol Records and the Beach Boys embarked on a path littered with hits. In June of 1962, "Surfin' Safari" rose to number fourteen, and the next year saw the release of another top-twenty hit, "Surfin' USA." There seemed to be a recurring theme in the songs, and the public did not show any sign of tiring of the surf songs, with "Surfer Girl" hitting the charts next. Jardine, realizing his mistake, returned to the group, ousting a reluctant Marks. The hits kept coming: "Fun, Fun, Fun," "I Get Around," "Dance, Dance, Dance," "California Girls," "Barbara Ann," and "Help Me Rhonda." In total the Beach Boys produced twenty singles that reached the top forty and twelve albums to grace the top-forty album chart.

The Beach Boys offered a unique sound to the rock 'n' roll scene, and songwriter Brian Wilson played the leading role in creating that sound. His early influences included Chuck Berry, the Ventures, and Phil Spector's "Wall of Sound." The often simplistic teen lyrics were counterbalanced by complex vocal harmonies. As the years went on, and Wilson began to experiment with increasingly technical musicality, the messages of the lyrics began to reflect the depth of the music itself. The 1963 ballad, "In My Room," particularly represents the scope of Wilson's talent. He took the group to a new musical level with the release of *Pet Sounds* and "Good Vibrations," which hit number one. The rigorous schedule of the group took its toll, and Brian Wilson suffered from mental problems and drug abuse. In the mid-sixties, Brian's participation in the band had diminished significantly, and the album *Smile* was abandoned, unfinished. Wilson was replaced on the bass first by Glen Campbell and then by Bruce Johnston.

Brian Wilson's departure was a blow to the Beach Boys, and by 1967 the rock 'n' roll tide had swept by their surfin' sound. The San Francisco hippies and the growing psychedelic scene had taken center stage, and the Beach Boys' 1968 offering, *Wild Honey*, was met with minimal enthusiasm. Although they had faded from their earlier fame, the Beach Boys continued to record, producing nineteen albums in the next twenty years. A few hits were sprinkled throughout the decades. In 1976, they hit number five with a remake of Chuck Berry's "Rock and Roll Music." And in 1988, their contribution to the soundtrack of the hit movie *Cocktail* reached the pinnacle of the charts. "Kokomo" was their first number one hit in well over twenty years. Later in that same year, the Beach Boys were inducted into the Rock 'N' Roll Hall of Fame.

Unfortunately, not all of the Beach Boys were able to experience the renaissance. The drummer

Dennis Wilson had spent his career to a certain extent in his older brother's shadow. Dennis had been a faithful and reliable member of the Beach Boys, but he contributed little to the group's artistic development. Without an individual claim to fame, the decline of the Beach Boys meant the decline of Dennis Wilson. Before he could ride the returning figurative wave of success, Dennis Wilson was downed by the literal waves of the Pacific Ocean. On the chilly evening of December 28, 1983, Dennis was puttering around on his yacht in Marina del Ray. In those evening hours, Dennis drowned near this boat, in the sea that had made him famous. Without more details, it is unclear whether this was a cruel twist of fate or whether Dennis took a more active hand in creating the irony. We do know that it was the golden sun and the crashing surf that gave the Beach Boys their niche in the world and rock 'n' roll and that it was the same surf that took Dennis Wilson to his grave.

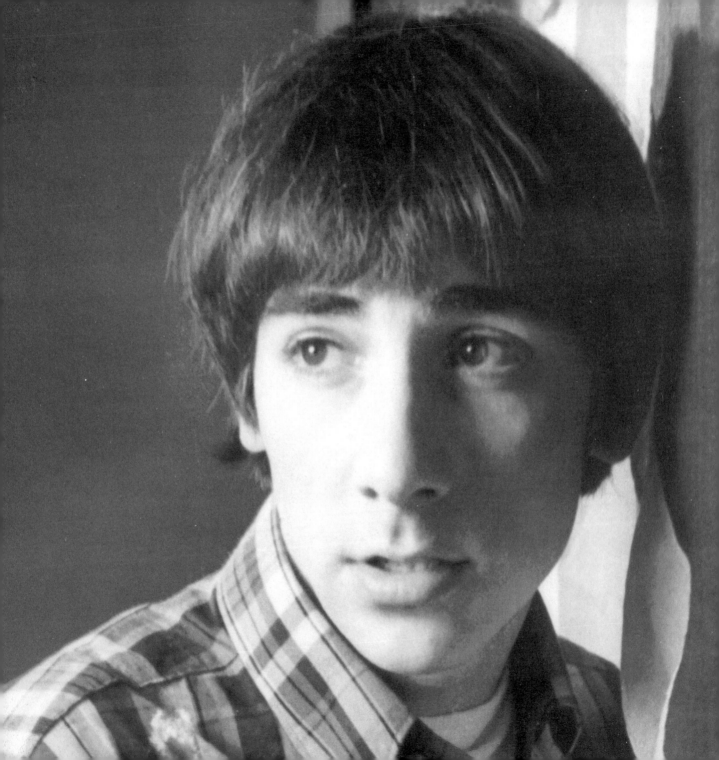

Chapter 10 .

The Longest Chapter

John Belushi

John Belushi is unrivaled in his conquest of three realms of entertainment—TV, film, and rock 'n' roll. He successfully remade himself again and again. Sadly, in trying to be so much to so many people, John Belushi lost himself.

John Adam Belushi was born January 24, 1949, in Wheaton, Illinois. His father was a hardworking Albanian immigrant who spent all of his time at his two restaurants, and John was raised primarily by his mother. At Wheaton Central High School, John was an extremely popular student and involved in everything—cocaptain of the varsity football team, all-conference middle linebacker, homecoming king, class clown, and an actor in the school shows.

John also had a passion for rock 'n' roll, and throughout high school he played drums with some friends in a band called the Ravens. Although the Ravens played only at school dances and youth center functions, they did make one record, "Listen To Me Now," paid for by a band member's father. The band sent the record to all of the local radio stations, but no one would play it and most of the hundred copies ended up as prizes for dance contests.

After graduation in 1967, John got his first professional acting job, doing summer stock theater in Shawnee. He enrolled at the University of Wisconsin in the fall but transferred the following year to the college of DuPage for financial reasons. During college, John and two friends formed a comedy group called the West Compass Players, eventually starting their own coffeehouse and hiring themselves as the entertainment. Their growing reputation led to an audition for the Second City Comedy Troupe in Chicago, and in February 1971 John was hired. Although he was only twenty-two, it was not long before John began to steal the shows and within a year it seemed inevitable that he would have to move on.

John's break came in 1972 when he was hired for *Lemmings*, a satirical off-Broadway revue produced by the *National Lampoon*. Belushi packed up and moved to New York City with his high school sweetheart Judy Jacklin. *Lemmings* was very successful, running for many months until John's performance began to suffer from his increasing drug use, primarily cocaine and Quaaludes. Still, Belushi continued to work on *National Lampoon* shows for the next few years, developing the concepts and working with the performers who would become the foundation of a new television show. On October 11, 1975, *Saturday Night Live* introduced a new brand of television, a weekly show broadcast live for the young and hip. Before long, John emerged as one of the show's rising young stars, but again he turned to drugs to maintain the brutal pace of the lifestyle.

Two years later, John's life grew even more hectic in October 1977 when he began filming *Animal House* in addition to *Saturday Night Live*, commuting between New York and Oregon every week. Belushi continued to take a leading role in *SNL*, and soon he had developed one of the most popular skits in the show's history.

For over a year, John and Dan Aykroyd had been doing an act called the Blues Brothers as a warm-up before *Saturday Night Live*, and on April 22, 1978, they incorporated it into the show. The bit went so well that it evolved into a semipermanent band of well-known session musicians who worked out an entire set of blues classics and dance routines. The project soon expanded into a movie for Universal, followed by a record deal with Atlantic. Elwood (Aykroyd) and Joliet Jake (Belushi) made their concert debut as the Blues Brothers on September 9, 1978, at Universal Amphitheater in Los Angeles and they were a smash. That same month, John also released his first solo record, "Louie Louie," on MCA followed by a debut album for the Blues Brothers. Recorded live during their Universal show, *Briefcase Full of Blues* went gold and then platinum. In January of 1979, the album hit the number one spot on the charts. The album also yielded a hit single; "Soul Man" reached number fourteen.

As Belushi fought to juggle three successful careers, it became common knowledge in the show business world that drugs were dominating his life. In an attempt to ease the pressure, John quit *Saturday Night Live* in 1979. He continued working and touring with the band, however, and soon began making movies such as *1941* and *The Blues Brothers*. The latter proved to be the pinnacle of Belushi's multimedia crossover success, earning $32 million in only two months. Although John tried several times to quit using drugs, the temptation was obviously too much. Fans were thrilled to give John drugs so they could party with a star, and Belushi's behavior began to spiral out of control. He became self-destructive and was often too strung out to perform, at times closing down an entire day's filming.

Near the end of 1981, Belushi's final film *Neighbors* was released, and the next month he returned to L.A. He moved into the Chateau Marmont Hotel to work on a script, but John ended up instead spending most of his time at the L.A. rock clubs, jamming with punk bands. On March 1, 1982, John met heroin addict Cathy Smith and she introduced him to a deadly combination. Cathy and John spent the next four days in his hotel room, doing coke and heroin until their days and nights became an endless party. On the fourth night they ventured out to a few different clubs and Cathy shot John up several times with a combination of heroin and cocaine called a speedball. It was early March 5, 1982, when they returned to the Chateau Marmont and John went right to sleep after one final shot. He woke up feeling cold, started to cough and choke, but then he stopped

and Cathy left at about 10:15 A.M. Returning a few hours later, Cathy found John Belushi dead from a drug overdose.

Cathy Evelyn Smith skipped off to Canada on March 15, 1983, but she was soon arrested and charged with second-degree murder and furnishing and administering cocaine and heroin. Her sentence was three years in prison.

On March 9, Dan Aykroyd led the funeral procession to Abels Hill Cemetery on Martha's Vineyard, Massachusetts, while James Taylor sang "Lonesome Road." Two days later, over 1,000 friends and relatives were at the memorial service in New York when Aykroyd kept his promise to John by playing a tape of "The 2,000-Pound Bee" by the Ventures.

Mike Bloomfield

Mike Bloomfield was a renowned session guitarist and an invaluable member of several bands. He was respected above all for his dedication to his art, though in the end his art was sacrificed to the drugs that also took his life.

Michael Bernard Bloomfield was born on July

28, 1943, in Chicago, Illinois, to an affluent Jewish family who raised him to take over the family business. Their plans hit a snag when Michael received a transistor radio for his bar mitzvah and discovered music, especially R&B and the blues. When Michael was thirteen, he started helping out in his grandfather's pawnshop and one day he brought a guitar home with him. Although his father was dismayed, Mike's mother, a former actress, was understanding and she arranged guitar lessons for him. Michael learned quickly and by the age of fifteen, the left-handed guitarist was playing with his own band. A dedicated blues disciple, Michael also started haunting Chicago's famed R&B clubs, learning firsthand from a multitude of legendary bluesmen. Before long, Michael was jamming with some of his idols, including Muddy Waters, Albert King, and Big Joe Williams.

By the time he was eighteen, Michael had garnered quite a reputation for his participation in numerous blues and folk sessions. He caught the attention of John Hammond, who flew to Chicago to see him. Hammond was impressed and signed Mike to the Columbia label. Soon Michael had recorded an album's worth of material, but because of a contract mix-up it was never released. In 1965, Mike was approached by Paul Butterfield, an old rival from the club scene, who asked Michael to join his group, the Paul Butterfield Blues Band. They started recording as soon as Michael moved to New York, but these sessions were also never released.

In July the band made music history with their infamous appearance at the Newport Folk Festival when Bob Dylan gave his first nonacoustic performance. Dylan played to a shocked folk community backed up by the electric guitars of the Paul Butterfield Blues Band. The band returned to New York to finish recording and then Michael took off for Woodstock, to play guitar on Dylan's album *Highway 61 Revisited*. The album included, among others, the classic, "Like a Rolling Stone." Bob Dylan offered Mike a permanent job, but Bloomfield decided to stay with the Butterfield Blues Band, which was scheduled to tour in October 1965. The tour was in support of their recent debut album, *The Paul Butterfield Blues Band*. The touring continued and was followed by a second album, *East West*, in August 1966. Life on the road proved to be too much for Michael, and he quit the group in 1967.

Mike Bloomfield returned to session work, playing with a variety of artists including Judy Collins, Mitch Ryder, and Peter, Paul and Mary. Looking for a fresh musical direction, Michael decided to move to California and put a new band together. The Electric Flag made its debut on June 16, 1967, at the Monterey Pop Festival. The band released *A Long Time Comin'*, its memorable first record in March 1968. The group recorded one more album, as well as the soundtrack of *The Trip*, before breaking up eighteen months after it was formed. In 1968, Michael started a series of collaborations that would continue for many years beginning with "Super Session" with Al Kooper and Stephen Stills. The next few years brought "Fathers and Sons" with Muddy Waters and "Triumvirate" with John Hammond and Dr. John. Mike at the same time worked on his own solo tracks, including "It's Not Killing Me" and "Analine." He also did soundtracks for *Steelyard Blues* and *Medium Cool.*

Drugs were a constant in Michael's life, and in the late sixties he began to lose himself to his heroin addiction. Reduced to making music for porno movies, he quit playing guitar, stopped going out, and withdrew into his drug seclusion. Periodically he would get clean and start working, only to return to heroin again and again. Eventually some of Mike's friends, including B. B. King and Carlos Santana, confronted him about the fact that his playing had deteriorated to the point of embarrassment. With such a wake-up call, Michael determined to kick the habit.

Michael rejoined Electric Flag for an unsuccessful attempt at reunion in 1974. In 1976, he entered his final band, KGB. Although he continued to release new records, sometimes two or three a year, Mike became increasingly irresponsible over the next few years, falling back to the use of drugs and alcohol. He encountered severe financial difficulties and had several run-ins with the IRS. Eventually he alienated the majority of his friends, colleagues, and even fans. Still, he tried for another reformation in 1980 when he swore off the toxins again.

Clean, sober, and engaged to soul mate Christy Svane, Michael seemed truly happy and 1981 got off to a great start. He recorded three albums' worth of material and released a new LP, *Living in the Fast Lane.* It looked like he was winning the battle with his demons when suddenly the demons got the better of him.

The mystery began the morning of February 15, 1981, in the Forest Hills section of San Francisco when the police discovered the body of John Doe number fifteen. Locked inside a 1971 Mercury parked on Dewey Street, the body was soon identified as Michael Bloomfield, thirty-six. His death was determined to be an accidental overdose caused by a combination of benzoleogonine, a morphinelike substance, and cocaine/amthamphetamine poisoning. While some of his friends accepted this verdict, others wondered about suicide, a heroin relapse, or even foul play. Many people still consider the death of Michael Bloomfield to be unresolved, but the truth will probably never be known.

Michael's service was held on February 18 at Sinai Memorial Chapel in San Francisco, and his ex-wife Susan, Bill Graham, and country singer Joe McDonald were among the mourners. On February 20, the body was flown to Los Angeles for a second service. Michael Bloomfield was buried at Hillsdale Memorial Park, 6001 W. Centinala Ave., Culver City, California.

Tommy Bolin

In 1976, Deep Purple made it into the *Guinness Book of World Records* as the world's loudest band. In addition to winning this distinction, Deep Purple impacted the world of rock 'n' roll by helping to bring the extravagance of hard rock into the mainstream. Known throughout the world for their jagged guitar riffs and clanging rhythms, Deep Purple left a lasting mark in the evolution of heavy metal. Had guitarist Tommy Bolin not overdosed on heroin, he would certainly be a mover and shaker in today's music scene.

Tommy Bolin was born in Sioux City, Iowa, in 1951 and learned to play the guitar at a young age. He got his first break with the James Gang and then moved across the ocean to join Deep Purple in April of 1975 when guitarist Ritchie Blackmore left to form his own band, Rainbow. Bolin's recording debut, *24 Carat Purple*, exploded onto the charts and shot up to number fourteen. "The Butterfly Ball," written by bassist Roger Glover, achieved attention as a single and was performed at the Royal Albert Hall in London.

The next album, *Come Taste the Band*, highlighted Bolin's courage and facility on the guitar and quickly entered the top twenty in England. The album charted in the United States as well, reaching number forty-three. A successful world tour followed, with stops in Britain, Europe, Asia, Australia, and the USA. This tour gave birth to the Guinness World Record as well as to a top-twenty album, *Deep Purple Live*.

At the close of the tour, in July 1976, Deep Purple split apart. The members went on to various careers, as solo artists and with other bands. Tommy Bolin returned to the United States to form the Tommy Bolin Band. This venture proved to be short-lived due to an unforeseen tragedy. On December 4, 1976, Tommy indulged in one too many shots of heroin. He died in his room at the Newport Hotel in Miami. Tommy Bolin was twenty-four years old.

Tim Buckley

In the nine albums he recorded between the years 1966 and 1974, Tim Buckley's innovative music pushed the boundaries of both sound and concept. Although his unique talent was passed over by the commercial music industry, his courage allowed for significant progress in the realm of jazz-rock and funk-rock fusion.

Timothy Charles Buckley III was born February 14, 1946, in Washington, D.C. His career began in Los Angeles where he performed with country-western bands as a solo player and guitarist in the early sixties. Making a name for himself as a singer/songwriter, Tim's versatile voice and eclectic style attracted the attention of Herb Cohen, Frank Zappa's manager. With Cohen behind him, Tim signed with Elektra Records in 1966 and released a self-titled debut album in October. Although well received by the critics, the folk-rock offering was a commercial failure that didn't make the charts. The year 1966 also saw the end of a brief marriage after the birth of a son Jeff in Anaheim, California, on November 17.

By 1967, Tim was in New York, playing with ex-Velvet Underground singer Nico. He released a second album, *Goodbye and Hello*, produced by Jerry Yester of the Lovin' Spoonful. Although the album contained his best known song, "Morning Glory" (covered by Blood, Sweat and Tears among others), it sold disappointingly. The following March he was on the opening night bill at the Fillmore East with Albert King and Big Brother and the Holding Company. Tim's career was on the upswing, with a UK tour, several television appearances, and the 1969 release of *Happy Sad*, a jazz-oriented album that reached number eighty-one on the U.S. charts.

In 1970, Tim's turn to jazz became more pronounced with the release of *Lorea*, an album consisting of an experimental free-form jazz style. The music was not especially listener-friendly and the album did not sell. In 1971, he put together *Starsailor*, a jazzy avant-garde experimentation which did not sell either, but which did yield one of his best known songs, "Song to the Siren." Disillusioned by the continued lack of capital success, Tim walked away from music for over a year. After a stint as a cab driver and a short tenure as Sly Stone's chauffeur, Tim returned to music to record *Greetings from L.A.* in 1972. The funk-rock album was well received critically but again failed to chart.

In 1973, Tim moved to Frank Zappa and Herb Cohen's DiscReet label. A successful European tour followed, including an appearance in the UK at the 1974 Knebworth Festival. *Look at the Fool*, another danceable funk offering was released, but the album was a failure both critically and commercially.

On June 29, 1975, Tim bowed out of the rat race. Always a partier, Buckley set off for a night of revelry at a friend's house in Santa Monica, California. He was expecting to party all night and he snorted what he believed to be cocaine early in the evening. It turned out to be a mixture of heroin and morphine, and the combination proved too much for Buckley's body to handle. By the next morning, at the age of twenty-nine, Tim Buckley was dead. With him went a wealth of untapped potential and wasted promise.

Marge Ganser

The Shangri-Las, the first girl greaser group, rejected poodle skirts and ponytails in favor of short skirts, tight shirts, and tall black boots. These were New York City girls, worldly and dramatic and ready to tell the world their stories of teen angst and young love. Among the most successful female groups in the early sixties, the Shangri-Las contributed several hits to the canon of rock 'n' roll.

These girls of teen melodrama were two pairs of sisters: Mary and Betty Weiss and twins Marge and Mary-Ann Ganser. All four attended St. Michael's Catholic School in Queens, where they formed a band and began to perform at school functions and other local gigs. They called themselves the Bon Bons and their debut recording was "Wishing Well." The single got little public reception, but it did attract the attention of producer George "Shadow" Morton. In 1964, Morton renamed the group the Shangri-Las and had the girls record his original song, "Remember (Walkin' in the Sand)." Recorded in a Long Island basement, this haunting ballad was the Shangri-Las' ticket to success, hitting number five on the charts. The hit gained them entrée into the inner circles of pop, and later that same year the Shangri-Las joined Marvin Gaye, the Searchers, and Martha and the Vandellas in a live series of performances at the Brooklyn Fox in New York. Mary Weiss, the youngest of the four, had to stay at school during this run.

Once the Shangri-Las had tasted sweet success, they became unstoppable. In October of 1964, they embarked on a tour of the United Kingdom, where they played to hordes of devoted teenaged fans. Upon their return to the U.S., the lineup shifted slightly again, as Mary replaced her older sister Betty Weiss. This pattern continued, with the Shangri-Las usually missing one of the original four and performing as a trio. November of 1964 saw the release of the group's biggest hit of their career, "Leader of the Pack." "Leader of the Pack" eventually reached the coveted number one spot in the U.S., but experienced a rockier road in the UK. The song was initially banned in Britain for its suggestive and rebellious lyrics!

Once the ban was lifted, "Leader of the Pack" went to number eleven on the UK charts. The song combined all of the elements that made the Shangri-Las famous. It was a narrative song, telling the story of a love affair with a boy from the wrong side of the tracks. It incorporated sound effects such as motorcycles and breaking glass, and the use of such sound effects soon became one of the group's signature techniques. "Leader of the Pack," like other Shangri-Las songs, had an autobiographical feel which elicited the empathy of teen audiences. The popularity of "Leader of the Pack" was proven again and again—in 1965 the Detergents made a parody of the song called "Leader of the Laundromat."

More hits followed "Leader of the Pack." "Give Him a Great Big Kiss" and "I Can Never Go Home Anymore" maintained the themes of rebellion, sex, and broken hearts. In "I Can Never Go Home Anymore," the Shangri-Las let down their tough-girl image, admitting this time that the parents were right. The next hit came in July of 1966 with "Past, Present, and Future." This innovative work was a confessional monologue spoken by Mary Weiss over the sounds of Beethoven's Moonlight Sonata. Hitting number fifty-nine on the American chart, it would prove to be the group's last top-100 offering. The girl group was being replaced by the more mature and serious sounds coming from the West Coast and from across the Atlantic.

The Shangri-Las did not die without a fight. Their hit "Leader of the Pack" was revived twice, hitting number three in 1972 and number seven in 1976. The group continued to play to enthusiastic crowds as they traveled the U.S. and the UK on various oldies tours. The decline was undeniable, however, and the individual members of the band dealt with their fall each in her own way. Marge Ganser made some destructive choices, and with the onset of the 1970's, she found herself hooked on various drugs. The problem worsened as the years went on, and in 1976 the chemicals that had initially provided a means of escape proved fatal. She was the first of the Shangri-Las bad girls to succumb, and her band mates and the music community at large mourned her passing.

Jimi Hendrix

Although Jimi Hendrix died before his musical vision could be fully realized, his legacy lives on as an inspiration to every hard rock and heavy metal band that exists today. Jimi often said that he couldn't play guitar well enough to get onto tape all the music he had in his head and felt in his heart. One can only imagine.

Jimi Hendrix was born November 27, 1942, in Seattle, Washington. Named Johnny Allen by his mother Lucille, the name was changed to James Marshall four years later by his father Al who had been away in the army at the time of the boy's birth. At age twelve James got his first guitar, a present from his father who had swapped his saxophone at a local pawnshop. Since he was left-handed, James turned the guitar upside down and played it backwards, a technique he continued throughout his career rather than playing a left-handed guitar. He taught himself to play by listening to the records of Robert Johnson, B. B. King, and other blues greats.

In 1959, a year after his mother's death, Jimi switched to electric guitar and joined a band called the Rocking Kings. Later that year, he enlisted in the army as a paratrooper, to avoid the draft. He was discharged several months later for medical reasons after breaking an ankle in a jump. After leaving the army, James adopted the stage name Jimmy James and entered the world of music. He played in numerous bands including Bobby Taylor and the Vancouvers, who later charted three singles with lead guitarist Tommy Chong.

Jimmy's talent was apparent and he easily secured work, touring as a sideman for, among others, Sam Cooke, Jackie Wilson, and Little Richard. His first significant audio work was on the Isley Brothers' 1964 single, "Testify."

In 1965 Jimmy formed his own group, Jimmy James and the Flames, playing R&B standards as well as original material at small New York clubs. It was during this time that he began experimenting with his instrument, adventurously expanding the musical boundaries with masterful manipulation of the wah-wah pedal, fuzz box, and Univibe. In 1966 he caught the eye of Animals bassist Chas Chandler at Greenwich Village's Club Wha?. Chandler, seeking management and production opportunities, whisked Jimmy to England and teamed him with bassist Noel Redding and drummer Mitch Mitchell. Chandler christened him "Jimi" and the Jimi Hendrix Experience was born.

Jimi created an immediate furor on the London pop scene, a flamboyant American who did not conform to anyone's idea of a black blues player. His physically aggressive avant-garde style made him not only a media darling, but made fans of the Beatles, the Rolling Stones, Pete Townshend, and Eric Clapton. On October 18, 1966, the Jimi Hendrix Experience played their first gig in support of French pop star Johnny Hallyday at the Paris Olympia. In January 1967, the single "Hey Joe" entered the UK charts. During the next fourteen months the band logged extensive studio time, recording singles "Purple Haze" and "Burning of the Midnight Lamp," as well as albums *Are You Experienced* and *Axis: Bold as Love*. "Purple Haze," with its allusions to mind-expanding drugs, became an anthem for the "love generation" and hit number three in the UK. *Are You Experienced* rose to number two on the British album chart, topped only by the Beatles' *Sgt. Pepper*.

At the insistence of Paul McCartney, the Jimi Hendrix Experience made their live U.S. debut at the Monterey Pop Festival, and Jimi's breathtaking rendition of "Wild Thing," which included setting fire to his Fender Stratocaster, brought down the house. The band's next performance, however, in support of the Mamas and the Papas at the Hollywood Bowl, was met with boos. The following month the band began a tour in Atlanta in support of the Monkees, but Jimi's music and showmanship were hardly a hit with the teenybop audiences, and they were pulled from the tour after only seven dates. Chandler used this to fuel a publicity stunt, claiming that protests from the right-wing Daughters of the American Revolution brought about the cancellation.

The next year saw arduous touring and a rapid rise to U.S. stardom, due in part to the success of singles "All Along the Watchtower" and "Foxy Lady." In October 1968 the double album *Electric Ladyland*, featuring performances by Al Kooper, Buddy Miles, and Steve Winwood, was released. Sexually explicit cover art caused some retailers to refuse to sell it, but the album still hit number one in the U.S. and number six in Britain.

In July 1969 both Redding and Mitchell quit the band, but a month later, backed by a group of musicians that included Mitchell, Jimi played Woodstock. His rendition of "The Star Spangled Banner" was the hit of the all-star two-day festival. Jimi was in fact the highest paid performer, receiving a fee of $125,000. Jimi's outrageous showmanship—playing guitar behind his head or with his teeth and sexually caressing the instrument made him the crowd favorite.

New Year's Eve marked the debut of Jimi's Band of Gypsies, a trio that included Buddy Miles and army buddy, bassist Billy Cox. The performance at the Fillmore East in New York was recorded and released as a self-titled album. On July 1, 1970, Jimi recorded his first session at his Electric Ladyland studio in New York. His musical style was setting a new standard for rock and inspired many jazz musicians to incorporate elements of rock, contributing to the rise of jazz-fusion.

In September a European tour was cut short for various reasons and Jimi looked for additional shows in England. On September 16, he joined Eric Burdon and War on stage in a London club in what would be his final public appearance. On September 18, Jimi Hendrix overdosed on barbiturates at the apartment of his girlfriend, Monika Danneman. After being rushed to St. Mary Abbot's hospital, Hendrix was pronounced dead due to vomit inhalation after barbiturate intoxication. Jimi is buried in the Greenwood Cemetery at the Dunlap Baptist Church in Seattle.

Shannon Hoon

Blind Melon could be seen as a one-hit wonder. But the group could also be seen as the ultimate in alternative music—a band that went about creating angst-ridden music, regardless of commercial success. Shannon Hoon was the driving force behind the group, and when they lost his careening vocals, Blind Melon lost its identity.

Shannon Hoon was born Richard Hoon in Lafayette, Indiana, in 1967. An all-American kid, Hoon turned from sports to music when he was in high school. He worked at singing and playing the guitar, and soon he was looking for a band. Although a band of his own was still a few years down the road, Shannon found work with a childhood friend—Axl Rose. Axl gave his friend his big break when he asked him to sing backup vocals on the Guns N' Roses *Use Your Illusion* album.

It soon became clear that Hoon's voice was not intended to stay in the background. After his sessions with Guns N' Roses, Shannon had the credentials to form a band. He started to jam with guitarist Roger Stevens and bassist Brad Smith, and in 1990 in Los Angeles Blind Melon was born. Brad Smith gave the band its name, after the nickname that unemployed hippies called each other in Mississippi. The Blind Melon sound combined the introspection of the alternative scene with the playful sound of the Woodstock era. Hoon's high-pitched vocals were the cement that held the music together, and his wails and screams inspired comparisons with Janis Joplin.

Blind Melon released their eponymous debut album in September of 1992. The album's claim to fame was its out-of-the-blue hit, "No Rain." This number one single was youthful and accessible, and its MTV video became as popular as the song itself. The video featured a young girl in a bee costume, and the band would later complain that the young actress got more interview time than they did. In spite of their complaints, Blind Melon actually spent several weeks at the top of the industry. They appeared—nude—on the cover of *Rolling Stone* in the spring of 1992. They played to sellout audiences and *Blind Melon* went gold.

In many ways, the fame went to Shannon Hoon's head. He flaunted all authority and made mischief wherever he went; he played Woodstock '94 in drag. His mischief took on a harder edge as well. He indulged in a variety of drugs, and his trips often included lewd and violent behavior. He was arrested in 1993 in Vancouver for stripping and urinating on stage. After losing the American Music Award for Best New Artist to Stone Temple Pilots, Shannon Hoon assaulted a security guard.

Late in 1994, Blind Melon entered a New Orleans studio to record their second album, *Soup*, for the Capitol label. This second offering failed to make the splash that the debut had, but the supporting tour was still a success. It seemed for a while, also, that Shannon had straightened up. He moved back to Lafayette with Lisa Crouse, his girlfriend of ten years, and their new baby daughter Nico Blue. Hoon had decided that it was time to settle down and accept the responsibilities of fatherhood.

The reformation did not last long. While touring, Shannon was arrested for drunk and disorderly conduct. The tour went on, and Shannon's debauchery continued. October of 1995 found the band back in New Orleans, just blocks from their recording studio. They had made a long trip from Indianapolis, and the band rested up in the tour bus. It had been an especially long trip for Shannon, spiced up with various drugs. At 1:30 P.M. on October 21, Blind Melon was ready to start warming up for their gig at the New Orleans Club Tipitina's. When Hoon failed to show up, the band sent the sound engineer to find him. He found him in the back of the tour bus, unconscious. At twenty-eight years old, Shannon Hoon had died of an accidental overdose.

Janis Joplin

J anis Joplin, one of the most successful white blues singers in the history of music, is a study in contrasts. Her public personality was one of parties and playfulness, while her private personality was one of pensiveness and pain. Her soulful sound bridged this gulf in her person and allowed her to find a few moments of peace in her short life.

Janis was born in Port Arthur, Texas, on January 19, 1943. A model child, she was artistic, smart, well-adjusted. She took art lessons, wrote poetry, and even skipped a grade. Janis' teen years weren't quite as happy—bad skin and a weight problem made her self-conscious and withdrawn. Beyond the normal teen woes, however, Janis began to feel a restlessness that isolated her from her peers. They could not understand or accept her unconventional views and lack of traditional feminine values, and Janis slowly became an outcast and the object of ridicule and abuse.

Janis was hurt by the rejection, but she found acceptance elsewhere, with a group of boys who were also outsiders. As "one of the guys," Janis shared with them an interest in beatnik intellect, adventure, and jazz and folk music. It was this love of music that led them across the state line to the Louisiana Honky-Tonks and introduced Janis to the music of Odetta. Janis soon discovered the blues, and blues great Bessie Smith became a major influence on her singing.

Janis graduated from high school in 1960 and entered Lamar College later that year. In college she divided her time between her studies and her music; she often left campus to sing in the clubs and bars of Houston and Austin. In the summer of '62, Janis moved to Austin and joined her first band, the Waller Creek Boys. She enrolled in the University of Texas, but the university students proved to be as intolerant as her high school classmates, electing her "Ugliest Man on Campus." Humiliated, she left Austin in a few weeks and hitched her way to California, arriving in San Francisco in January 1963. The San Francisco scene was tolerant and accepting, but Janis was still haunted by memories of her earlier torments and could never completely overcome her insecurities.

Only when she was singing did Janis feel truly at ease, and soon her performances—solo or with Jorma Kaukonen (Hot Tuna)—began to attract attention. Possessing a three-octave range, Janis sang with abandon, pouring her soul into the music with a heart-stopping intensity that won her acclaim in the music scene. She approached the free love and drug scenes with the same abandon; she was open to anything. Janis' lifestyle began to spiral out of control. Splitting her time between San Francisco and New York, Janis developed a speed addiction while continuing to drink heavily. When her weight got down to eighty-five pounds, Janis decided it was time to return to Port Arthur and straighten up. She went back to college, spent the next year getting her life back together, and was about to join the 13th Floor Elevators when an old friend convinced her to come back to San Francisco and join a new band.

Janis made her debut with Big Brother and the Holding Company in June 1966, and just a year later they stopped the show at the Monterey Pop Festival. In August, Mainstream released their eponymous debut album, which was received with critical respect. Soon, the ambitious band got a new manager, Albert Grossman, and a new deal with Columbia. In 1968 Big Brother exploded with the album *Cheap Thrills* which went straight to number one. Janis was the key to the success, with her hits "Down on Me," "Piece of My Heart," and "Ball and Chain." Driven by her own personal popularity, Janis quit Big Brother before the year's end, and less than a month later she made her first appearance with a new band backing her.

In the midst of her meteoric rise to fame, Janis had gotten into heroin, and though the constant touring and recording helped to keep it under control, it started to affect her performance by the time she played Woodstock. After Woodstock live shows continued to flounder, but Janis' first solo record, *I Got Dem Ol' Kosmic Blues Again Mama*, was released in September 1969 and rose to number five on the charts. Janis was riding high, in more ways than one.

The spring of 1970 saw Janis swear off heroin. She quit her most recent in a long string of bands, and after a reunion show with Big Brother in April, she debuted her new group, the Full Tilt Boogie Band, in May. The band spent the next few months touring, and in September they arrived in Los Angeles to start recording their first album. Everything seemed to be full steam ahead—Janis was making wedding plans, she was happy with the band, and the album was almost finished. Then suddenly Janis fell off the wagon and returned to her days of syringes and lost nights.

On October 4, 1970, Janis Joplin stopped at

Barney's Beanery after a recording session and had two screwdrivers before returning to her hotel, the Landmark. The vodka entered her bloodstream on top of the extremely pure heroin that she had shot into her veins hours before. Her body could not take the onslaught, and Janis had taken only a few steps into Room #5 when she fell face-first and died. Her death was ruled an accidental overdose. People still in shock over Jimi Hendrix's death just two weeks earlier were left to ponder the similarities. There was a private service for family members on October 7 at the Westwood Village Mortuary in Los Angeles, and then Janis' body was cremated and her ashes scattered along the Marin County coastline.

Released several months after her death, Janis' final album *Pearl* was another hit and contained her first number one single, "Me and Bobby McGee." Since her death there have been several books written about Joplin, the film *The Rose* based loosely on her life, a memorial in her hometown, and several retrospective record releases.

Paul Kossoff

Although Paul Kossoff was essentially a fun-loving boy until the day he died, his talent and innovation have established him as one who could have been one of the guitar greats. Unfortunately, his exceptional party skills cut short his career, and his life. We can only guess at the music that Paul Kossoff may have created had he lived out his potential.

The son of well-known English actor David Kossoff, Paul Kossoff was born September 14, 1950, in London. He came to resent his family's comfortable lifestyle while growing up, and as a young teen Paul dropped out of school and moved out on his own. He began to devote all his time and energy to music, and by the time he was seventeen Paul was playing guitar in an R&B band called Black Cat Bones. It was there that he met drummer Simon Kirke. In early 1968, Kossoff and Kirke happened to see Paul Rogers perform with Brown Sugar at a London club. Impressed by his explosive vocal energy, they invited Rogers to join them in forming a new band. A few weeks later they added bassist Andy Frazier, recently let go by John Mayall's Bluesbreakers, and the four musicians set out in search of a venue.

In May of 1968, the band, christened Free, debuted at the Nags Head in Battersea. They took advantage of the blues-rock trend that was sweeping Britain, and it was soon obvious that their sound had real popular appeal. In November, when the band signed a deal with Island Records, the company wanted to change their name to the Heavy Metal Kids, but Free refused to change. They released their debut album, *Tons of Sobs*, which failed to chart in the UK but made number 197 in the U.S. a year later. Even though Free's follow-up single "Broad Daylight" also failed to chart, the band soon began to acquire a large following due to nonstop UK touring. Their British popularity led to a U.S. tour in support of Blind Faith, a move which gave them much-needed American exposure. They reaped the rewards of the increased exposure when their next album, *Free*, charted at number twenty-two in November. In July, the single "All Right Now" hit number two in the UK and number four in the U.S.

Paul's understated guitar style was the cornerstone of Free's popularity. He had a manner of distilling blues down to riffs that established a unique sound and paved the way for later successful bands such as Bad Company and For-eigner. A hit album, *Fire and Water*, that contained "All Right Now" as well as a show-stealing performance at the Isle of Wight Festival seemed to put Free on the road to becoming a supergroup.

However, in spite of the fame and musical maturity, Free was still a very young group. After "All Right Now," disappointing follow-up releases "Stealer" and "Highway" heightened friction among the band members and led to a 1971 breakup.

Reforming in January of 1972, Free reached number nine in the UK and number sixty-nine in the U.S. with their June release of the album *Free At Last*. Paul missed several tour dates as his drug and alcohol problems began to escalate. In October, he officially left the band and recorded *Back Street Crawler*, his first solo album. The album was released in late 1973, and Paul soon formed a band with the same name, but his new career proved to be tragically short-lived. In the summer of 1975, Paul Kossoff's drug use led to a massive heart and lung stoppage, rendering him officially dead for thirty-five minutes until doctors could manage to revive him. The following year, he was not so lucky, and on March 19, 1976, on a flight from Los Angeles to New York, Paul Kossoff died of drug-related heart failure. He was twenty-five years old.

Phil Lynott

P hil Lynott was an only child, born into a Brazilian/Irish family on August 20, 1951, in Dublin, Ireland. His parents split up when he was five. Raised by his grandmother, he considered himself a misfit and developed what he called "a bit of the robber spirit." It had always been his mother's intention to come back and take charge of the boy, but it never happened. When Phil was sixteen, he started playing bass in a cover band called the Black Eagles with boyhood chum, drummer Brian Downey. When Phil and Brian added Eric Bell from Belfast on guitar, Thin Lizzy was born.

By late 1970, Thin Lizzy had developed a local reputation as a strong performance band, drawing the attention of a Decca A&R man who eventually signed them. The label moved the band to London where they made little or no impact playing club gigs. April of 1971 saw the release of their self-titled debut album which failed to chart. The following year, *Tales from a Blue Orphanage* also failed, but the 1973 single "Whiskey in the Jar," a rock version of an old Irish folk song, was a surprise hit, rising to number six in the UK.

A good portion of Thin Lizzy's material was based around a mixture of fighting songs and tough guy adventurism. Even the love songs found basis in these themes. Thin Lizzy's one top-forty hit was the number twelve "The Boys Are Back in Town," a single released from the album *Jailbreak*. Although he was not an overwhelming commercial success, Phil Lynott deserves credit as a forerunner of the punk movement. After the dissolution of Thin Lizzy, Lynott played with Rat Scabies of the Damned, Midge Ure of Ultravox, and the Rich Kids.

Phil Lynott always followed his own path in life, and though his influence was not wide, it was deep and it greatly affected the evolution of punk and post-punk sounds. In his lifestyle, however, Phil Lynott followed the basic rules of rock stardom—take drugs, lots of them. A series of overdoses put Phil into a coma at the end of 1985, and on January 4, 1986, Phil Lynott died of a drug-induced heart attack.

Keith Moon

Keith Moon's fiery drumming was integral to the success of The Who. Off stage, however, Moon's primal sensibility often got the best of him.

Keith Moon was born in Wembly, London, on August 23, 1946. The son of a mechanic and a cleaning lady, Keith attended Harrow Tech and became a trainee electrician. In his free time, he played a mean set of drums with a surf band called the Beachcombers. This first band gained him entrée into the world of music, and one night Keith showed up out of nowhere at a Detours gig and demanded to sit in with the band. Surprisingly enough, they let him, and soon the Detours had a new member. Keith's wild style immediately clicked with band mates Pete Townshend, John Entwistle, and Roger Daltrey.

The Detours changed their name to The Who for a short time in 1964 until manager/publicist Peter Meaden suggested the High Numbers, a name fitting with the mod image. Soon after, film directors Kit Lambert (son of noted composer Constant Lambert) and Chris Stamp (brother of actor Terence Stamp), who were planning a documentary on London's blossoming mod subculture, saw the High Numbers in concert. Seeing a vast potential for stardom, the directors bought out Meaden's interest for 500 pounds.

One night at Harrow's Railroad Hotel, the neck of Pete Townshend's guitar broke off on the low ceiling. The crowd roared with excitement, inspiring Townshend and Moon to destroy everything on the stage. Soon, the band became known not only for their unique rock sound but also for the flagrant destruction of their equipment. Lambert and Stamp were quick to figure out that this destruction was a key to the future popularity of the group. Word soon spread and crowds arrived weekly to witness the mayhem, enabling Lambert to secure the band a regular Tuesday night gig at London's famed Marquee Club. They were billed as The Who—Maximum R&B. The Marquee Club performance led to an appearance on the British television show *Ready, Steady, Go,* where Pete and Keith smashed and demolished not only their equipment but the set as well. The Who rose to immediate fame.

The band was a hit, quickly becoming Britain's third biggest rock 'n' roll act behind the Beatles and the Rolling Stones. In 1965 their debut single, "I Can't Explain," hit the UK charts at number eighteen and the American charts at number ninety-three. Their debut album, *My Generation*, reached number five on the British album charts. The year 1966 saw an appearance on ABC's popular *Shindig*, a tour with the Spencer Davis Group, and a change in management as Allen Klein and Andrew Oldham took over for Lambert and Stamp. In May of that year, Townshend and Daltrey went on stage with a stand-in bassist and drummer at the Rikki Tik Club in Newbury when Entwistle and Moon failed to show up. When Keith and John finally did arrive, Townshend hit Moon over the head with his guitar during "My Generation," causing a black eye and a cut leg. Keith quit the band but rejoined days later.

In 1967, The Who released *Happy Jack* and *Pictures of Lily*, the latter reaching number four in the UK under the new Lambert/Stamp label, Track Records. The band received major notice at the Monterey International Pop Festival and then embarked on their first US tour, supporting Herman's Hermits and the Blues Magoos. Following the tour, The Who played the Hollywood Bowl as "I Can See for Miles" cracked the U.S. top ten.

Major success followed in 1969 with the release of the rock opera *Tommy* and a performance at Woodstock that captured the imagination of the youthful generation. The year 1971 saw the release of the album, *Who's Next*, the band's first UK chart topper (U.S. number 4). In 1973 the rock opera *Quadrophenia* rose to number two on both sides of the Atlantic. The ensuing years featured synthesizer orchestrations, sold-out stadium gigs, and numerous side projects. Keith had small parts in several movies, including *Tommy*; Frank Zappa's *200 Motels*; David Essex's rock films, *That'll Be the Day* and *Stardust*; and Mae West's *Sextette*.

Though several punk bands listed The Who as being influential, the advent of punk in the late seventies left Pete Townshend in a midlife crisis which eventually led to the breakup of the band. "Who Are You," the last hit featuring the band's original lineup, was inspired by a drunken brawl between Townshend and Paul Cook and Steve Jones of the Sex Pistols.

Keith Moon was the soul of The Who's live performances. He was a brilliant drummer who brought a passionate intensity to the stage, highlighted by a thunderous, slamming style and the dramatic accents of classical percussion. But it was his flamboyant performances off stage for which "Moon the Loon," rock's favorite lunatic, became legendary. "There was a time in Saskatoon, in Canada," Keith recalled for *Rolling Stone*:

It was another Holiday Inn, and I was bored. Now when I get bored, I rebel. I said "Fuck it. Fuck the lot of ya!" And I took out me hatchet and chopped the hotel room to bits. The television, the chairs, the dresser, the cupboard doors, the bed—the lot of it. Ah-ha-ha-ha! It happens all the time.

Later, Keith took to destroying rooms methodically, quietly taking apart furniture and rearranging the room to give the appearance that it had been ransacked.

Always the practical joker, Moon frequently used itching powder and cherry bombs. He also loved to dress up. Often he assumed the persona of a proper English gentleman, a nun, or even Adolf Hitler. His antics sometimes went way beyond the pale of good taste, as evidenced by the time that he and Viv Stanshall of the Bonzo Dog Band dressed up as Nazis and paraded up and down the primarily Jewish Golders Green section of London.

At a Flint, Michigan, Holiday Inn during The Who's first American tour, Keith was presented with a huge birthday cake which he proceeded to hurl at the throng of well-wishers. A major food fight ensued and everyone had a great time until the manager returned. He was less than amused by the sight—his carpet trodden with marzipan and his guests dancing about with their pants down. Keith ran out and jumped into the first car he saw, a new Lincoln. When he released the parking brake, the car started to roll and, as a non-driver, Keith sat helpless as the car rolled down a hill, smashed through a fence, and landed in a swimming pool. Sitting at the bottom of the pool

with the water pouring through the windows, Keith could not get the door open. With the water reaching his nose he took a gulp of air, then managed to push open the passenger door and swim to the top of the pool. Expecting a crowd to have gathered, Keith was disappointed to see that the only person there was the pool cleaner.

A more tragic turn behind the wheel occurred in 1976 when Keith tried to escape a crowd of rowdy skinheads outside a disco in Hertfordshire. Desperate to get away, he jumped into his Rolls Royce and backed over his chauffeur, Cornelius Boland, killing him. Sadly, Moon disregarded the circumstances and his surroundings and was able to make the court laugh as he pleaded guilty to drunk driving. All other charges were dropped.

Keith's alcohol and drug use was legendary, as he frequently partook of these toxins until he blacked out. He did not remember recording the song "Substitute," and when he heard it on the radio he was convinced that The Who had replaced him with another drummer. In 1977, Moon found himself in Los Angeles where he engaged in perpetual drinking contests with Ringo Starr and Harry Nilsson while recording a disastrous solo album. The following year he returned to London and took residence in Nilsson's expensive Mayfair flat (the same flat where Cass Elliot had died in 1974). Moon was tired, overweight, and aged beyond his years.

On September 8, 1978, Keith and his girlfriend Annette Walter-Lax attended a midnight matinee of *The Buddy Holly Story*, then went to a party thrown by Paul McCartney at the fashionable Peppermint Park restaurant. They returned home around four A.M., and Keith had trouble sleeping. He rose for an early breakfast, then went back to sleep with the aid of thirty-two Heminervan tablets. It was more than twice the lethal dosage of these pills used to battle alcoholism. At 3:40 the next afternoon Annette awoke to find Keith dead beside her. Keith Moon's body was cremated on September 11, 1978, and a small private funeral was held two days later.

Gram Parsons

Gram Parsons was an individual who took his vision and his musical integrity with him wherever he traveled. A defining member of both the Byrds and the Flying Burrito Brothers, Parsons contributed his country-western influences to the development of both bands.

Cecil Connors was born on November 5, 1946, in Winterham, Florida. When he decided on a career in music, he decided to change his name to the showier Gram Parsons. Talented on the keyboards and the guitar, Gram did stints with several minor bands before he heard that David Crosby and Gene Clark had left the Byrds. The Byrds were pioneers in the world of folk-rock and as such were major forces in the evolution of rock 'n' roll in the 1960's. Known to many as the "American Beatles," the Byrds were famous for their electric versions of folk classics. In 1965, the Byrds grabbed the number six spot on the charts with their album featuring an electric version of Dylan's "Mr. Tambourine Man." The following year they had two top-forty albums: *Turn! Turn! Turn!* hit number seventeen and *Fifth Dimension* held the number twenty-four slot.

In March of 1966, Gene Clark departed and the look of the band changed; Clarence White and Vern Gosdin came aboard in the guitar section and the South African trumpeter Hugh Masekela offered his expertise. Undaunted by the lineup changes, the Byrds continued to churn out the hits. The single "So You Want to Be a Rock 'N' Roll Star" rose to number twenty-nine on the charts and was characterized by an increased jazz influence. *Younger than Yesterday* was released the same year and featured another successful remake of a Dylan song, "My Back Pages." As the year went on, internal changes were in the works. McGuinn changed his name from Jim to Roger, most likely to satisfy the wishes of his Subud cult. David Crosby departed soon after and left the door open for Gram Parsons.

Gram Parsons joined the Byrds and immediately began to make his vision known. With Chris Hillman, Parsons coaxed the group toward his enthusiasm for country-rock fusion. The Byrds performed at the Grand Ole Opry—a testament to the deep influence that Parsons had on the group. His influence spread into the recording studio as well, the Byrds went to work on *Sweetheart of the Rodeo*. The album would be the first truly country-inspired work done by a rock band. Other groups had approached the genre; the Beatles, the Rolling Stones, and the Buffalo Springfield had all experimented with the country sound, but none had committed to the extent that the Byrds did. Bob Dylan released his own fusion album, *Nashville Skyline*, after *Sweetheart of the Rodeo* was in the record stores.

Ironically, by the time *Sweetheart* came out, Gram Parsons had left the Byrds. He took the moral high ground, refusing to tour in South Africa, and consequently quit the group in July of 1968. After Parsons left the Byrds, his vocals on *Sweetheart of the Rodeo* had to be rerecorded in order to satisfy contract requirements. The Byrds suffered greatly from Parsons' departure, and without their guiding light, they floundered in the realm of country-rock fusion. Soon Chris Hillman also left the group to join Gram Parsons in his new endeavor.

In this new group, Parsons found a fresh vehicle for exercising his country-rock vision. The Flying Burrito Brothers grew to define the California version of country-rock, combining the country-western sound with bluegrass and Latin influences. Gram Parsons, handling vocals, guitar, and keyboards, was joined by Hillman on bass and vocals, Sneaky Pete Kleinow on the pedal steel guitar, Jon Corneal on drums, and Chris Ethridge on the bass. Parsons was the driving force behind the group, and when he departed from them, the Flying Burrito Brothers faded from view.

It was September 19, 1973, when Gram Parsons departed from the Flying Burrito Brothers and from the world of the living. A heroin user for many years, Parsons overdosed at his home in Joshua Tree, California, and died on that September evening. It seemed that some were not ready to let him go, for a few days later Gram's coffin was stolen from the L.A. airport by hijackers dressed as funeral home employees. Phil Kaufman, a longtime roadie for Parsons, later admitted to the crime. He told authorities that he had set the body on fire on a stone called Cap Rock, which had apparently been one of Parson's favorite places. The roadie claimed to have been carrying out Gram's wishes, but rumors flew about a cult sacrifice. Regardless of the reason, it is certain that Gram Parsons left this world in a blaze of glory, just as he would have wanted.

Elvis Presley

Elvis Presley was without a doubt the king of rock 'n' roll. In many ways he was also its father—the father of the mystique, the image, and the hype that is now as integral to the world of rock 'n' roll as the music itself. Elvis Presley was a symbol to the youth of America: he was young, he was energetic, his music was intoxicating. A newly formed teen culture rallied behind him as their representative. He sang of young love and broken hearts, and every teenager in his audiences thought that he was singing to her, or about him. Elvis' following of devoted fans was unprecedented in the music industry, and the following did not diminish after his death. Graceland has become the destination of many a pilgrimage and stands as a testimony to the contributions of "the King."

Elvis was born on January 8, 1935, in the small town of Tupelo, Mississippi. Eighteen years later, on July 18, 1953, Elvis began his music career by recording a private record at Memphis Recording Service. Elvis' youthful potential attracted the attention of studio owner Sam Phillips, for whom Elvis recorded a remake of Arthur Crudup's "That's All Right Mama." And so it began. Elvis' sound was a new mixture of country-western, rhythm and blues, and gospel, and the combination was a winner. Soon Elvis was crooning to the crowds at state fairs and coming over the airwaves on local radio stations. Even in these early stages, Elvis had an electrifying effect on audiences, and soon he had made a name for himself in the southern country music circles. In July of 1955, Elvis' single "Baby Let's Play House" hit number ten on the Billboard Country charts and this success led to an RCA contract in November of 1955.

"Heartbreak Hotel," which came out in April

of 1956, was the King's first major hit. It rose to number one and catapulted Elvis into the national spotlight. He began making TV appearances—*The Stage Show, The Milton Berle Show, The Ed Sullivan Show*—backed by guitarist Scotty Moore, bassist Bill Black, and drummer D. J. Fontana. On the *Ed Sullivan Show*, the cameraman was instructed to film only Elvis' face—not his hips—during his on-air performance, as Elvis' free-spirited gyrations were deemed inappropriate for the television audience. With his slick hair, his slick suits, and his active pelvis, Elvis turned many heads, both in condemnation and near worship. In 1956 Elvis' superstardom was established. "Heartbreak Hotel" was followed by fellow number one singles, "Don't Be Cruel," "Hound Dog," and "Love Me Tender." Two albums also reached the pinnacle of the charts, *Elvis* and *Elvis Presley*, and Elvis branched out into film, signing a $450,000 three-movie contract. *Love Me Tender* came out in 1956 and was a smash hit.

Elvis' Midas touch continued into the next year, with number one singles "Too Much," "All Shook Up," "(Let Me Be Your) Teddy Bear," and "Jailhouse Rock." This last was accompanied by a blockbuster film of the same name. *Loving You* and the *Elvis Christmas Album* rose to the top of the album charts, and Elvis reigned supreme in rock 'n' roll. In March of 1958, Elvis was drafted into the army, but Elvis' fame did not fade when he donned the uniform. RCA had held some of his singles and both "Don't" and "Hard-Headed Woman" hit number one while Elvis was overseas

serving his country. Later that year, tragedy struck when Elvis' mother Gladys passed away.

Elvis couldn't be kept down, however, and as soon as he was discharged in 1960 the King went back to work and soon churned out two more number one singles, "Stuck on You" and "It's Now or Never." The year 1961 saw the release of three more number one hits: "Are You Lonesome Tonight," "Surrender," and "Good Luck Charm." As the sixties unfolded, Elvis began to turn more and more to Hollywood, and his movies were always commercial, if not critical, hits. The soundtracks also did well on the charts, but by the mid-sixties Elvis was forced to pass his crown on to the newcomers of the British Invasion. Although he receded from center stage, Elvis continued to perform, on stage and in front of the camera. In 1968, a television special, *Elvis*, put him back into the public eye, and in 1969 Elvis released his final hit, "Suspicious Minds."

The Elvis Presley of the late sixties and seventies was a far cry from the fresh-faced boy who charmed the audiences of the fifties. In many cases, he was still playing for the same fans, who had aged along with him, but to keep them interested, Elvis became more and more outlandish in his costumes and demeanor. Satin and spangles had replaced the sleek look of the early days, and the flabby king was now a caricature of his former self. Elvis had been swept along by the demons as well as the angels of fame, and it was the demons that determined the path of his lifestyle. Ex-bodyguard Red West was quoted by Harry Surall as saying that Elvis was "a walking pharmaceutical shop who took pills to get up, pills to go to sleep, and pills to go out on the job."

Hooked on amphetamines and barbiturates, Elvis poisoned his body relentlessly while struggling to maintain a clean public image. He was in fact a public crusader against drug abuse, and he persuaded the Federal Bureau of Controlled Substances to give him an agent's badge. He kept several guns in his house which he had earmarked for use against drug dealers. The conflict between his public persona and the inner reality must have intensified the pain of a declining career and a losing battle against substance addiction.

On August 16, 1977, Elvis Presley died. The official cause of death was heart failure, but the reality behind the story was, again, much more complicated. Elvis was one hundred pounds overweight and suffered from hardening of the arteries, heart disease, diabetes, and a perforated colon. Traces of eight different drugs were found in his body. The reality is that Elvis died of his groundbreaking fame, of his unexpected fortune, of trying to be too much to too many people. He has now become a cult figure, inspiring thousands of impersonators and afficionados. It is interesting to note that the impersonators focus on his later period, on the years of degeneration and inner turmoil. Perhaps it is an appropriate tribute to the paradoxical, decadent, and ultimately destructive world of rock 'n' roll.

Hillel Slovak

The original Red Hot Chili Peppers were fast—they played their guitars fast, they drove fast, and they lived fast. It took the death of one of their founding members, Hillel Slovak, to get them to slow down—not speed up—at the yellow lights.

Hillel Slovak was born in Haifa, Israel, on April 13, 1962. Within five years, his family was forced to move to America to escape the threat of impending war. They lived in New York for a short time before settling in Los Angeles. Hillel felt like an outsider in L.A. until he became friends with Jack Irons and discovered a shared passion for music. The two boys idolized KISS and spent hours listening to and talking about music. They eventually staged their own performance, miming KISS shows with costumes, makeup, and fake blood. As Hillel's interest in music got more serious, he started taking guitar lessons, and a short time later formed his own band, Chain Reaction, with Jack and two other friends. The band later became Anthym and then, What Is This, with a new bass player known as Flea and an MC, Anthony Kiedis.

Calling themselves "Los Faces," the band members were close friends and classmates at Fairfax High School. Soon Anthony and Hillel discovered that they shared an interest in drugs as well as a love of music. After graduating in 1980, the band drifted apart for several years and Hillel played with James White.

In April 1983, a friend asked Flea and Anthony to put together an anything-goes act for a one-time performance, to open his show in the Rhythm Lounge. They recruited Hillel and Jack and wrote a song called "Out In L.A.," which they didn't even rehearse for their brief appearance as Tony Flow and the Miraculously Majestic Masters of Mayhem. They were on and off stage in less than five minutes, but it was so explosive that the crowd went wild and the manager immediately asked them to return for another show. After changing their name to the Red Hot Chili Peppers, the band began to rehearse, writing one or two more songs for each show, which they would round out with a cappella campfire songs. A few

short months later, the band that had started as a joke was opening for Run DMC.

The Red Hot Chili Peppers were constantly exploring different kinds of music and trying new combinations of sounds, senses, and musical influences as they started to develop their own unique style. The band began to get a reputation for their intense live shows, a mixture of sex, energy, frenzied mayhem, and loud, fast music. The free-for-all attitude carried over into their personal lives, as Hillel and Anthony continued to experiment with drugs. By November 1983, within six months of their first show, the Red Hot Chili Peppers signed a contract with EMI. The deal did not include Hillel and Jack, who decided to stay with What Is This and a deal with MCA.

What Is This released their first record in 1984, the "Squeezed" EP, followed by *What Is This*, featuring a remake of the Spinners' "I'll Be Around," which became a minor hit in the summer of '85. In spite of the promising start, Hillel soon jumped ship and rejoined the Red Hot Chili Peppers. By spring, the group was in Detroit with producer George Clinton, recording their second album. *Freaky Style* was released in September and the band was on the road a month later, touring continually in the U.S. and Europe until March 1986, when they took a break and accepted Jack into the fold. It was like old times, but the "sex, drugs, and rock 'n' roll" lifestyle was taking its toll on Hillel and Anthony. They were both hooked on heroin and their addiction was snowballing out of control.

The group seemed to be falling apart, but they continued on, touring and recording their third album, *The Uplist Mofo Party Plan*. Although Hillel tried to hide his drug addiction, he became increasingly isolated and his playing started to deteriorate. When the music began to suffer, the band tried to convince him to straighten up. He went clean and stayed clean for a while, but when the band returned to L.A., Hillel returned to heroin. Less than two weeks after returning to the West Coast, Hillel had his last fix.

It was Saturday, June 27, 1988, when Hillel Slovak overdosed on heroin, alone in his apartment. At the age of twenty-six, he fell into a coma that night and died. His body was discovered on Monday and he was buried the next day following a memorial service at Mount Sinai Memorial Park in Los Angeles. In Hillel's death, Anthony finally found the courage to overcome his own long battle with drugs. The inspiration of his songs "Knock Me Down" and "My Lovely Man" is a testament to the memory of Hillel and the love and friendship that he and Anthony shared.

Sid Vicious

Some have said that the Sex Pistols represent the greatest commitment to the antiestablishment ideal in the history of rock 'n' roll. Their punk edge, both musical and ideological, spearheaded a youth subculture that exists to this day. Sid Vicious led the reckless charge, racing along at a pace that could only destroy him.

Sid Vicious was born John Simon Ritchie on May 10, 1957, in London, England. Sid lived in southeast London until he was three and then he went to Ibiza with his mother Anne for a lengthy vacation. Sid's father was supposed to join them or send money, but he never did either, so Sid and his mother returned to England when they ran out of funds. Abandoned and in debt, Anne moved in with her mother and began a new life. Soon Sid and his mother were doing much better—she found a job and they got their own place. Anne loved music, especially jazz, and she passed this love on to her son.

Following the early troubles, Sid had a fairly normal childhood until he started at Hackey College of Further Education and met John Lydon, better known as Johnny Rotten, who gave his life a new dimension. It was Lydon who gave Sid his new name, Sid Vicious, after a pet white rat, and the two became the best of friends. The punk scene was just starting up in London, and Sid and John were soon swept up into it. It was on King's Road at Malcolm McLaren's shop that they met a new group called the Sex Pistols. Steve Jones (guitar), Paul Cook (drums), and Glen Matlock (bass) had originally been called the Swankers, but they had gotten rid of their singer along with their name. After getting to know John, they gave him an audition and hired him. Although Sid was jealous of John's new position, he became the Sex Pistols' biggest fan and attended all their shows. Sid was credited with the invention of "the pogo" when the frenzied jumping that he called dancing evolved into a punk craze.

By the summer of 1976, the Sex Pistols were playing every Tuesday night at the 100 Club in London, and in September they headlined at the 100 Club Punk Festival. Siouxie and the Banshees made their debut at the festival with Sid playing drums, but their twenty-minute performance of "Knocking on Heaven's Door" and "Twist and Shout" did not go over well with the audience. Sid left the group soon after the first show. While Sid was playing in different groups, including the Flowers of Romance, the Sex Pistols signed a record deal with EMI, released their first album, *An-archy in the UK*, and lost their record deal. In the process they became one of the most notorious rock bands ever, for their wild behavior on and off the stage. The band fired bassist Glen Matlock in February 1977 and hired Sid, fulfilling his dream of becoming a Sex Pistol. They signed a new contract with A&M on March 9, 1977, and though they were dropped a week later, A&M released a limited number of their single "God Save the Queen."

Even though he had achieved his goal, Sid could not control his habits, and after a trip to Berlin he was admitted to the hospital with hepatitis from drug misuse. He signed the group's new contract with Virgin on May 16, the day he was discharged. "God Save the Queen" was the Sex Pistols' first record on Virgin, but because of the typically controversial cover and content, nobody wanted to press the record or print the sleeve. The single was finally released on May 27, but the problems continued. The song was banned by the BBC and many record stores refused to sell it. Still, it sold over 150,000 copies in less than a week and made it to number two on the UK charts a few weeks later.

The Sex Pistols' next two singles, "Pretty Vacant" and "Holidays in the Sun," both made the top ten, but as their fame grew, so did their reputation for trouble. The Sex Pistols were sued over the picture on a record cover and they could only play in the UK under a fake name. On October 28, the Sex Pistols released their eagerly awaited album *Never Mind the Bollocks—Here's the Sex Pistols*. The album awakened a new round of controversy, including a court case to decide if "bollocks" was obscene. This time the stores which did not ban the album were the target of police raids to confiscate the records. Eventually, the courts ruled that it was legal to display and sell the album, and nothing could stop the Sex Pistols from holding the number one spot on the charts.

By this time, Sid and his girlfriend Nancy Spungen were continually harassed by the police, and when the couple was arrested on drug charges in December, the band decided that Nancy was a bad influence on Sid. Partially to keep Sid away from her, the band spent the rest of the year touring. They returned to England just before the holidays to play a charity show for children on Christmas day. Soon they were off on their first (and last) American tour, and they left Nancy at home. The Pistols' itinerary consisted of seven shows with the first one on January 5, 1978, in Atlanta, Georgia, followed by Memphis, Baton Rouge, Dallas, and Tulsa. The tour was going badly, the band was unhappy, and Sid was worthless. It was the last straw when he fell down five times during the final show in San Francisco. When the Sex Pistols walked off that Winterland Ballroom stage, it was for the last time.

The Sex Pistols broke up for good following a huge fight after the show in San Francisco. John, Paul, and Steve all left town immediately, leaving Sid to fend for himself. A few days later, Sid overdosed on methadone during a flight from Los Angeles, and immediately after his arrival in New York he was hospitalized and enrolled in a detox program. When he was released, Sid and Nancy went to Paris to work on the Sex Pistols' movie, *The Great Rock 'n' Roll Swindle*. Sid also recorded "My Way" before going back to London in the spring. In London, he recorded two more songs, "C'mon Everybody" and "Something Else." Sid put together a band with Glen Matlock called the Vicious White Kids but it fell apart after one show.

Sid and Nancy decided to relocate to New York and moved into the Chelsea Hotel at 222 West 23rd Street during the last week of April 1978. Nancy was now managing Sid's career and booked some shows for him at Max's and CBGB, but the jobs stopped coming when people saw that Sid could not even remember his own songs. For both Sid and Nancy, heroin was out of control and their life completely revolved around finding the next score. They hardly left their room except for drugs—they didn't even think to leave when they accidentally set their room on fire. They often spoke of death as their lives were falling apart. We will never know if Sid's death was a self-fulfilling prophecy or a plan.

On October 12, 1978, Sid and Nancy made one of their rare excursions from room #100 of the Chelsea Hotel. They went shopping and bought two new knives and a large quantity of heroin—a deadly combination. Later that night, Nancy was found in the hotel room, stabbed to death. It is unknown whether the drug dealer returned and stabbed her or if Sid and Nancy made a suicide pact or if it was simply a horrible accident. When the police arrived, Sid was heavily drugged and oblivious to what had happened. He did tell the police that he had not killed Nancy, but his fingerprints were on the knife and so Sid was arrested.

The next morning, after being charged with second-degree murder, Sid was taken to Riker's Island and put into detox. The tabloids went crazy, and Nancy's death gave her the kind of sensational front-page attention she would have loved. Sid tried to kill himself and he even asked the New York police to kill him, saying that he could not live without Nancy.

In November, Sid was released on $30,000 bail and soon he had a new girlfriend, Michelle. Within a few weeks, however, he was back in jail after a bar fight. When Sid was released again, his mother and Michelle picked him up and took him to Michelle's apartment in the Village to celebrate. He had been clean for several months, and his body was unprepared for the large amount of pure heroin that he shot into his veins that night. Sid Vicious, age twenty-one, was found dead from an overdose on February 5, 1979.

Andrew Wood

Andrew Wood was a pioneer of the grunge scene who did not live long enough to see its explosion into the mainstream. His band, Mother Love Bone, gave birth to the blockbuster group Pearl Jam, and Eddie Vedder picked up the crown where Wood dropped it.

Mother Love Bone was among the first to streamline the grunge sound into a slightly more accessible sound, with the help of heavy blues in-fluences. In 1984, guitarist Stone Gossard joined bassist Jeff Ament to found one of the first grunge groups in Seattle, under the name Green River. Green River signed onto the indie label Sub Pop, and their most successful album was *Rehab Doll*. The limited success was not enough to keep the group together, and Green River disbanded in 1988.

Gossard and Ament, along with drummer Jeff

Turner, were determined to stay on the grunge scene and soon they hooked up with vocalist Andrew Wood. Wood brought with him a more bluesy sound, and Mother Love Bone was born. Mother Love Bone expanded the definition of grunge with its blues influences and the technical scope of its members.

Unfortunately, the story of Mother Love Bone is more one of potential than of chart successes or legendary tours. The group recorded two albums on the Stardog/Polydor label: *Shine* in 1989 and *Apple* in 1990. Both received critical and popular admiration, but Mother Love Bone was destined to die after the release of the second album. Before *Apple* hit the record stores, Andrew Wood injected one too many viles of heroin into his young body. Wood died in 1990, but his legacy lived on and grew with the grunge revolution. Gossard and Ament moved on, producing music in various guises until they teamed up with Eddie Vedder later that year. The rest is Pearl Jam history.

Chapter 11

Together Beyond the Grave

The Allman Brothers Band
Duane Allman and Berry Oakley

The Allman Brothers Band's rise through the ranks of rock was based largely on Duane Allman's virtuosity on the guitar. Berry Oakley drove the rhythms on his bass and, together with four other talented musicians, Duane and Berry made a lasting name for themselves in the annals of rock 'n' roll.

Although Duane Allman was only twenty-four years old when he died, his accomplishments as a guitar player are legendary. He was born Howard Duane Allman on November 20, 1946, in Nashville, Tennessee. During the Korean War, Duane and younger brother Gregg lost their father, a sergeant in the U.S. Army, when he was murdered while on Christmas leave. Not much is known of this mysterious death. In 1959, Duane's mother relocated with her sons to Daytona Beach, Florida, hoping to begin a new life.

In high school, Duane and Gregg started their first band, the Kings, before working with, among other numerous bands, the Shufflers, the House Rockers, and the Y-Teens. Forming the Allman Joys in 1965, the brothers played countless bars throughout the South until they got the chance to record their first single, a remake of Willie Dixon's "Spoonful" for the Dial label. When the record was poorly received, several members of the band departed. The grinding schedule and lack of progress had resulted in the dissolution of the band.

In 1967, Duane and Gregg picked up some new musicians, renamed themselves the Hourglass, and moved to Los Angeles. Just a few months later, they signed a contract with Liberty Records. Closing out the year, they made their album debut with *Hourglass*, and then immediately returned to the studio to start recording their next LP. The band finished recording two more albums, but only one was released before they broke up.

The brothers returned to Florida and played with two local bands: the 31st of February and Second Coming. The two soon split up and Duane went out on his own, moving to Muscle Shoals, Alabama, to become a session guitar player. For the next year he played with many great musicians, including Aretha Franklin, Boz Scaggs, Wilson Pickett, King Curtis, and Percy Sledge. Earning the respect of these artists, Duane established himself as an up-and-coming session player.

Then, in early 1969, Duane returned to Nashville to spend time at home. He got together with some local musicians he knew from 31st of February and Second Coming and they started to jam—the six musicians clicked. They had Duane (guitar), Gregg (keyboards, vocals, guitar), Dickey Betts (guitar, vocals), and drummers Butch Truck and Jaimo Johanson. In the final spot was bassist Berry Oakley, born April 4, 1948, in Chicago. They called themselves the Allman Brothers Band.

The Allman Brothers Band moved to Macon, Georgia, and began touring steadily. In late 1969, the group finished its debut album, *The Allman Brothers Band* under the Atco label. Although Duane continued his session work—playing with Eric Clapton on the timeless Derek and the Dominoes piece "Layla," the band maintained an in-

tense touring schedule. In 1970, the nonstop touring began to pay off with the release of the band's second album, entitled *Idlewild South*, which hit number thirty-eight and became the Allman Brothers' first chart record. In 1971, the band recorded their Fillmore East shows on March 12 and 13 for their third album. This live double LP hit the stores in September and quickly rose to the top ten. The record went gold, and the Allman Brothers Band was on its way.

Less than a month later, on October 29, 1971, everything fell apart. Near dusk in Macon, Georgia, at Bartlett Street and Hillcrest Avenue, Duane lost control of his motorcycle in an attempt to avoid a peach truck. Three hours later, Duane Allman died on the operating table at Middle Georgia Medical Center.

At the funeral at Rose Hill Cemetery in Macon, Georgia, Eric Clapton and Dr. John played a few of Duane's favorites with the rest of the Allman Brothers' Band.

Deciding to carry on without replacing Duane, the band began to pick up the pieces. At the time of his death, Duane had completed several tracks for a new album. Leaving Duane's parts intact, the band finished the record and named it *Eat a Peach*. Released in February 1972, the record soon became another massive hit for the group.

But at two P.M. on November 11, 1972, tragedy struck again. Just three blocks from the site of Duane's fatal crash, Berry Oakley lost control of his motorcycle and hit a Macon City bus head-on.

Berry drove home after the accident, refusing medical treatment even though his helmet was cracked and blood was dripping down his neck. An hour later, his friends carried him into the hospital, but it was too late. He died a short time later from severe brain injuries.

Berry and Duane are buried side by side on Carnation Ridge at Rose Hill Cemetery.

Badfinger
Tom Evans and Peter Ham

Badfinger's accessible sound won them leagues of devoted fans, and the Beatles counted themselves among these admirers. The two groups collaborated on several projects, but in spite of their illustrious partners, Badfinger was destined to be wracked by tragedy.

Pete Ham was born in Swansea, Wales, on April 27, 1947. As a young boy, Pete learned to play the guitar and the piano, and in the mid-sixties he formed the Iveys with some kids from town. For the first couple of years, the band played mostly one-nighters, doing teen shows at youth clubs around southern Wales. In spite of the small scale of their gigs, the Iveys began to establish quite a following and gain notice from some names in the music industry. Former band leader Bill Collins was impressed enough to sign on as their manager, and singer David Garrick often used them as his backup band. The shows with Garrick kept the Iveys together and working steadily until their rhythm guitarist left in 1968. The Iveys filled the hole with Tom Evans. Born in the Liverpool on June 6, 1947, Evans had come from another struggling band, the Calderstones.

Newly armed with Evans, the Iveys began to enjoy some minor recognition after appearing on Garrick's single, "Dear Mrs. Applebee." The band soon secured several club dates in London, and at one of these shows they were discovered by the Beatles' road manager, Mal Evans. Mal gave a copy of their demo tape to Paul McCartney, and the Beatle liked what he heard. In July 1968, Mc-

Cartney signed the Iveys to his newly formed record label, Apple Records.

Four months later, the Iveys made their Apple debut with the single "Maybe Tomorrow," but it was released only in Europe, with mild success. In December, the band fired their bassist, switched Tom over from rhythm, and became a permanent quartet. The following September, they changed their name to Badfinger and began recording four songs for the soundtrack of an upcoming Peter Sellers/Ringo Starr film, *The Magic Christian*. One of the singles from the film, "Come and Get It," was written and produced by Paul McCartney and put Badfinger into the top ten for the first time. With the help of McCartney's name, the song reached number four in the UK and number seven in the U.S. Badfinger maintained a close relationship with the Beatles throughout their Apple association and worked together on several projects. Badfinger had a hand in such creations as "All Things Must Pass" (George Harrison), "It Don't Come Easy" (Ringo Starr), and "Imagine" (John Lennon).

Badfinger embarked on its first U.S. tour in the fall of 1970. The tour was a success, and the band followed it up with an album, *No Dice*, which yielded several hit singles. After a short hiatus, the band returned to the recording studio and emerged with another hit, "No Matter What." The song went to number eight in the U.S. and number five in Britain, and in August they appeared at one of the biggest all-star shows of the year, George Harrison's "Concert for Bangladesh." Harrison

soon returned the favor when his production of "Day After Day" became Badfinger's third top-ten hit. The single stayed on the charts (U.S. number four, UK number ten) for weeks and became the band's first gold record.

Meanwhile, Badfinger originals were enjoying success with other artists as well—a Harry Nilsson cover of the Ham/Evans song, "Without You" hit the charts and propelled Nilsson to fame. As Nilsson skyrocketed past Badfinger, the band produced its final hit single, "Baby Blue." After a few more unsuccessful recording ventures, Badfinger bowed out of Apple in search of a new start with Warner Brothers Records.

Although the Warner Brothers debut was a disappointment, within a year Badfinger had bounced back to make a strong start with their second album. Steady sales put them back on track as "Wish You Were Here" slowly climbed the charts. Sadly, the revival was short-lived and dissolved into chaos as the band uncovered serious financial fraud attributed to American manager Stan Polley. When Warner Brothers discovered the corruption, the album was pulled from record store shelves all over the country. By the time the band's name had been cleared and the issue settled, Badfinger had lost their momentum and could not recover.

Badfinger tried to press on, but their new recording attempt was stymied by enduring conflicts and the bad blood of the past. Pete's professional woes were supplemented by personal problems. In early 1975, Pete quit but returned several days later to try to resolve his problems. The band met to discuss its revival, but the plans were evidently not enough to convince Peter. On April 23, 1975, Pete Ham hanged himself in the garage of his Surrey home, just days before his twenty-eighth birthday. His girlfriend, Ann, found his body next to a suicide note that seemed to blame manager Polley for ruining his life.

Ham's death was the final nail in the coffin for Badfinger. Tom Evans continued to record with a group called the Dodgers, but this group soon collapsed, and in 1977 Evans took a job working as a draftsman. A year later, Badfinger was reincarnated when Evans joined with Molland, another original member, to record an album in 1979. After Badfinger signed with Radio records, another album followed, and the single "Hold On" made it to the number fifty-six spot in the United States. The band remained minorly successful for a few more years, but in 1983 Badfinger split up for good. Tom began to fight a legal battle for the rights to his songs, but it was a long, hard road. While the lawsuits continued, the stress mounted and he developed a serious drinking problem. Tom's financial situation became critical, and on November 18, 1983, the burden grew too heavy. At the age of thirty-six, Tom Evans hanged himself in his Surrey home, ending his life just as his fellow band member had less than ten years before.

Bob Marley and the Wailers
Bob Marley and Peter Tosh

Bob Marley and the Wailers were the masters of reggae; they introduced the world to the indigenous sounds of Jamaica and influenced generations of rock, punk, and pop musicians. Marley was a symbol of integrity in the music industry and an embodiment of unity and pride to the Jamaican people. He was a dedicated Rastafarian, and his dreadlocks and red, yellow, and green colors became idioms of popular culture. With Peter Tosh and Bunny Wailer, Marley spread the simple 4/4 rhythms, intonated vocals, and expressive guitar, as well as the live and let live reggae philosophy, into the mainstream of the rock 'n' roll world.

Bob Marley was born on February 6, 1945, in Nine Miles, Rhoden, St. Anne's, Jamaica. The son of a Jamaican mother and an English army captain father, Bob was educated at the Stepney School. It was at school that he met Peter Tosh (né Winston Hubert MacIntosh) and Bunny Wailer (né Neville Livingstone), and the three soon discovered their mutual love of native Jamaican music. In 1961, Marley recorded his debut single, "Judge Not (Unless You Judge Yourself)," for the Jamaican Beverley label. This first attempt, as well as the second single, "One Cup of Coffee," failed to attract attention, but Marley persisted.

The year 1964 saw the birth of the Wailin' Wailers, a reggae band consisting of Bob Marley, Peter Tosh, Bunny Wailer, Junior Braithwaite, and Beverly Kelso. After signing with the Studio One label, the group recorded the single, "Simmer Down," which sold over 80,000 copies in Jamaica and introduced the Wailers' name into music circles. The Wailin' Wailers recorded several more singles over the next few years, all of which were successful on the island of Jamaica.

In 1966, Bob Marley's life took several new turns. He married Alpharita Anderson and soon after the wedding set sail for the United States to join his mother. Marley got a job in a Chrysler fac-

tory but soon became dissatisfied with the lack of music in his life. He returned to Jamaica to rectify the situation, and in 1967 he formed the Wailin' Soul record label. His first artist was Johnny Nash and for his second act he signed himself. The new band was a trio, with Tosh and Wailer, and was to be known as the Wailers. The group began to work with producer Lee Perry and soon released "Soul Rebel" and "Small Axe" under their own label (now entitled Tuff Gong). The singles attracted local attention but failed to give the Wailers the break that they sought.

Although they had yet to produce a major hit, the Wailers spent their early years productively, developing their style and honing their technique. Their reggae had elements of calypso, rock 'n' roll, as well as the philosophical influence of the Rastafarian religion. Bob Marley was the undisputed leader of the group, both musically and ideologically. Peter Tosh was younger and, to many, more abrasive, and his rebelliousness would contribute to the identity that he developed later in life as a solo performer. Bob Marley and Peter Tosh were both controversial for their Rastafarian endorsement of marijuana as a means of moving closer to God. In spite of this objectionable stance, Marley was hailed by the Jamaican people and government as a national hero and was awarded Jamaica's Order of Merit.

The seventies proved to be the decade of success for Bob Marley. In 1972 the Wailers initiated a profitable partnership with Island Records. The group expanded to include Carlton Barrett on drums and Aston Barrett on bass. The new ensemble put out two albums in 1972—*Catch a Fire* and *Burnin'*—and the following year toured Britain as an opening act for Sly and the Family Stone. Just as the Wailers were getting up to speed, however, Peter Tosh and Bunny Wailer left the group because of disputes with the record company. As a result the Wailers changed its look and its sound, as the two deserters were replaced by three female vocalists: Rita Marley, Judy Mowatt, and Marcia Grifiths. The next few years saw the release of the successful album *Natty Dread* in 1975, and the hit single "Roots, Rock, Reggae," which hit number five on the U.S. chart in 1976. That same year, Eric Clapton's cover of Marley's "I Shot the Sheriff" went to the top of the charts. But 1976 was a year of extremes; Marley was beaten up on stage and diagnosed with cancer. The cancer was removed from his toe in a Miami hospital and Marley returned to the recording studio, this time to produce *Exodus*, an album that would reach the top twenty in the U.S. in 1977.

For the next two years, Bob Marley toured the world, spreading his music and his message across the United States and Europe. Near the end of the tour, in 1980, Marley collapsed on stage and soon learned that he had been living on borrowed time. After being rushed to the hospital, Marley got the word that his cancer had returned and that this time it was incurable. Marley's planned tour with Stevie Wonder was canceled and his career came to a screeching halt. Just months later, on March 11, 1981, Bob Marley succumbed to the dis-

ease. As a recipient of the Order of Merit, Marley was given a state funeral.

After Jamaica's favorite son was buried, the renegade son continued to create music and scandals. Peter Tosh had always been the most publicly outspoken of the Wailers, composing the more political material such as "400 Years," "Stop That Train," and "Get Up Stand Up." Soon after the Wailers dissolved, Tosh was inexplicably arrested and beaten by the Jamaican police. His debut solo single "Mark of the Beast" was a protest against police brutality and was immediately banned from the radio. His next release, "Legalize It," was also banned, but the censorship did not prevent its wide exposure and appreciation. Peter Tosh continued the crusade for the legalization of marijuana throughout his career, and at one performance he went so far as to smoke a joint on stage. Tosh proceeded to condemn Prime Minister Michael Marley's stance on the legalization issue. It just so happened that the Prime Minister himself was in the audience; it is unclear whether Tosh was aware of this. After the show, Tosh was arrested and again beaten to within an inch of his life.

Always resilient, Tosh recovered from the injustice and looked across the Atlantic for his next opportunity. The break came when he signed on to the Rolling Stones' label, Rolling Stones Records. His association with the Stones flourished and he opened for them on their 1978 tour of the United States. Mick Jagger and Peter Tosh recorded a duet, a remake of the Temptations'

"Don't Look Back," and Tosh and Jagger appeared together on *Saturday Night Live*. Peter enjoyed the notoriety that came with his connection to the Rolling Stones, but he maintained his political and social ideals. In 1981, he released *Wanted Dead and Alive*, a political commentary and musical masterpiece dealing with governmental corruption and social injustice. Tosh continued to produce albums with a conscience; his last was the peace tract, *No Nuclear War*.

On September 11, 1987, three well-dressed men entered Peter Tosh's home in St. Andrew, Jamaica, and opened fire. Their 9mm pistols took the lives of Peter Tosh, his chef Wilton Brown, and local DJ Jeff Dixon. Tosh's girlfriend Marlene Brown and four others were wounded before the murderers fled the scene. The reason for the massacre is unknown, but speculations range from drug trafficking to political revenge.

The Grateful Dead
Keith Godchaux, Ron McKernan, Brent Mydland, and Jerry Garcia

If the flower children, the me-generation of the seventies, the mine-generation of the eighties, and Generation X in the nineties had to agree on one musical hero, there can be little doubt that that hero would be Jerry Garcia. His fans span the political spectrum, from Bill Clinton to Strom Thurmond. When Jerry died on August 9, 1995, three generations lost a hero—a symbol of peace, love, playfulness, and ultimately, recklessness.

With the chance of survival at 25 percent, playing keyboards with the Grateful Dead has become one of the top five most dangerous professions known to man. Ron "Pigpen" McKernan was born September 8, 1945, in San Bruno, California; Keith Godchaux was born July 19, 1949, in San

Francisco; and Brent Mydland was born October 21, 1952, in Munich, Germany. All three played keyboards for the Grateful Dead and all three met with early demises.

Jerry Garcia was born in San Francisco to a Spanish jazz musician and a nurse. In a flash of premonition, his parents named him after songwriter Jerome Kern. Jerry's early childhood was a happy one; but then tragedy struck when a father-son fishing trip turned into a nightmare. While nine-year-old Jerry looked on in horror, Mr. Garcia was pulled under the water and drowned. This early brush with despair would provide a poignant counterpoint to the smiles in Jerry's music.

Jerry was not destined for a normal childhood. He dropped out of high school when he was sixteen and enlisted in the army the following year. After two court martials, it became clear that the military life fit Jerry no better than high school had. Jerry returned to San Francisco and finally found his niche—in music.

In the early sixties guitarist Jerry Garcia played the San Francisco coffeehouse circuit before forming the Wildwood Boys and later the Hart Valley Drifters, who won an amateur bluegrass contest at the Monterey Folk Festival in 1963. Soon after, he started jamming with Robert Hunter, future Dead lyricist, Bob Weir on the rhythm guitar, and drummer Bill Kreutzmann. The result of the sessions was Mother McCree's Uptown Jug Champions.

The evolution of the band, which grew to include Pigpen on harmonica, was fairly rapid, and they went electric soon after Dylan did. The Jug Champions became the Warlocks, and in 1965 they played with the Jefferson Airplane at Bill Graham's first rock show at the Fillmore Auditorium. By June 1966, the Warlocks, featuring Jerry, Pigpen, Bob Weir, Phil Lesh and Bill Kreutzmann, had become the Grateful Dead, a name they borrowed from a traditional folk tale. The Dead set up shop in a communal house at 710 Ashbury Street, the epicenter of the emerging hippie scene. They quickly gained a reputation as a band of the people, often playing benefits and free shows including several in Golden Gate Park.

In January 1967 Warner Brothers signed the Grateful Dead, and the band released a self-titled album in May. Recorded in only three days, the album featured Pigpen's trademark gruff blues-based vocals but none of the energy the band displayed on stage. It did, however, chart at number seventy-three and continued to sell consistently for several years, eventually going gold. In June, along with Jimi Hendrix and The Who, the Grateful Dead was one of the main attractions at the Monterey Pop Festival, though disagreements with industry executives caused them to be left out of the documentary film of the historic event.

Two more albums and performances at major festivals, culminating with an appearance at Woodstock in August of 1969, helped the Grateful Dead develop both an estimable musical reputation and legions of devoted fans. The band hit their recording stride in 1970, opting for a vocally rich country-flavored sound as albums *Working-*

man's *Dead* and *American Beauty* became critical as well as commercial successes.

The Dead enjoyed indisputable recording and commercial success, but their true claim to fame will always be their concerts—and the Deadheads. Jerry tried to explain the Deadhead phenomenon, telling Rolling Stone in 1983, "It is this time frame's version the archetypal American adventure. It used to be that you could run away and join the circus . . . or ride the freight trains." The first official fan club was started soon after the Dead came into existence; the three-member club called itself "The Golden Road to Unlimited Devotion." The grateful Grateful Dead took the name as a song title on their first album. Another organization, "The Church of Unlimited Devotion," went so far as to require a vow of celibacy of its members. The members of this "church" were called "Spinners" and were recognizable by the whirling-dervish dance that they did at the Dead shows.

The band utilized an extended family of musicians, including a second drummer, Mickey Hart, and keyboardist Tom Constanten, and took little time out from constant touring and prolific recording. In 1971, Pigpen, a heavy drinker, fell ill with a liver ailment and his appearances on stage became intermittent. To cover his absences, the group took insurance in the form of keyboardist Keith Godchaux. Pigpen's improving health allowed him to rejoin the band for the 1972 European tour, but on March 8, 1973, Ron "Pigpen" McKernan died of a stomach hemorrhage at his Marin County apartment, the direct result of liver disease.

Keith Godchaux became a permanent member of the Grateful Dead as did his wife Donna, a former Muscle Shoals session vocalist. The remainder of the decade saw the interchanging of personnel, a variety of individual side projects, label changes, continued recording and vigorous touring to sold-out venues which included a memorable series of benefit shows under the stars in front of the Great Pyramid near Cairo, Egypt, in 1978. In 1979 the Godchaux's were asked to leave the band due to musical differences. Keith was replaced by keyboardist Brent Mydland, who had toured and recorded with Bob Weir.

On July 21, 1980, Keith Godchaux was seriously injured when his car collided with a flatbed truck near Marin County, California. He died two days later. This tragedy, along with Jerry's heroin addiction, slowed the band slightly in the mid-eighties, but soon the Grateful Dead rebounded as active as ever. Philanthropy became more prevalent as the years passed, and the band donated their services for the benefit of dozens of causes, including Vietnam Veterans Project, Greenpeace, and Rainforest Action Network.

The Grateful Dead did not blaze any new musical trails during this period, but nonetheless their worldwide fan support grew. Armies of Deadheads, many of them in their teens, began following the band from city to city, attending every concert on any given tour. The year 1987 saw the Dead's first major hit single, "Touch of

Gray," which rose to the top of the charts. In June 1990 the band celebrated twenty-five years together, but the mood changed the following month.

On July 26, Brent Mydland died from an acute cocaine and narcotic intoxication (an overdose of morphine and cocaine) shortly after 10:30 A.M. at his Lafayette, California, home. He was survived by his wife Lisa and his daughters Jessica and Jennifer.

Grammy-winning keyboardist Bruce Hornsby helped out his old friends during this difficult period by filling in several dates including a five-night stand at New York's Madison Square Garden. Soon after, former Tubes keyboardist Vince Welneck signed on as a permanent replacement for Mydland.

The Grateful Dead kept on truckin', through tragedy and triumph, until the granddaddy finally stepped off. The Dead had replaced keyboardist after keyboardist, but there would never be a replacement for Jerry. It was August 9, 1995, that Garcia's hard living caught up with him. He had been in and out of rehabs, on and (mostly) off the wagon all his life. His fast-paced lifestyle epitomized the boyish spirit that made him who he was. The fun was destined to eventually catch up with him, however, and in 1986 he fell into a coma for the first time. He swore off heroin and cocaine for a while, but soon he was hooked again. He entered rehab again in 1994, after collapsing in his home. He was in rehab when his heart finally gave out. After years of drug abuse, Jerry Garcia died of a heart attack. He left behind four daughters, two ex-wives, and his current wife, filmmaker Deborah Koons. Jerry's death left his army of devoted fans in shock, and as they said good-bye, they knew that they had witnessed the end of an era.

Lynyrd Skynyrd
Ronnie Van Zant, Steve Gaines, Cassie Gaines, and Allen Collins

Lynyrd Skynyrd was the number one name in 1970's southern rock. Although they have numerous hit singles and albums, they will be remembered most of all for their high energy and feel-good live performances.

Ronnie Van Zant (January 15, 1949), Gary Rossington, and Allen Collins were students at Robert E. Lee High in Jacksonville, Florida, when they first met in 1965. Through school and sports, the three soon became close friends. A mutual interest in rock 'n' roll led to the formation of their first band, My Backyard, with Van Zant on vocals and Rossington and Collins both playing guitar. Although none of them had any musical experience, they slowly improved as they learned together. For the next several years, the band rehearsed as much as possible, though band members came and went almost as often as the name changed. Throughout this time period, the band played any job they could find and released two singles but failed to attract the attention of the record labels.

The group finally settled on the name Lynyrd Skynyrd. The unusual name was a takeoff on Leonard Skinner, their high school P.E. teacher who was known for his hatred of long hair. Van Zant, Rossington, and Collins had all been at various times suspended from school because of this particular antipathy.

The turning point for the band came in 1972 when the ever changing lineup finally stabilized and Lynyrd Skynyrd took to the road. They were "discovered" by Al Kooper while playing a club in Atlanta. Kooper signed them to MCA's newest label, Sounds of the South, and became the producer of their first album. The band's 1973 debut, *Pro-*

nounced *Leh-nerd Skin-nerd*, featured their unique three guitar southern rock sound and did fairly well on the charts. This album included "Freebird," which was written as a tribute to Duane Allman and soon became their trademark and an anthem for a generation.

Over the next four years, Lynyrd Skynyrd produced several gold albums, including *Second Helping* and *Nothing Fancy* along with hit singles "Saturday Night Special" and "Sweet Home Alabama." As their popularity increased, Lynyrd Skynyrd came to be considered one of the premiere southern boogie bands of the seventies. Still, the band personnel continued to change as members left, often as a result of their intense touring schedule or of their well-deserved reputation for general rowdiness.

In spite of the unrest, the core lineup remained constant until the arrival of three female backup singers, including Cassie Gaines, in 1976. In June of that year, the band also welcomed a new guitarist, Cassie's brother Steve Gaines.

Lynyrd Skynyrd's constant touring had made them one of the top concert draws in the U.S. in the 1970's. They took advantage of this acclaim with the release of *One More for the Road*, a live double album that took them to platinum land for the first time. The follow-up to this success was the band's sixth album, *Street Survivors*. This one was released on October 17, 1977, and a few days later, Lynyrd Skynyrd began a major U.S. tour to support their newest album.

The band left Greenville, North Carolina, on October 20, 1977, en route to Baton Rouge, Louisiana. They were traveling in a single engine Convair 240 that did not have enough gas in the tank, and the plane ran out of fuel eight miles from the airport and crashed into a swamp near Gillsburg. Ronnie Van Zant, Steve Gaines, Cassie Gaines, road manager Dean Kilkpatrick, and two other crew members died at a nearby hospital. The rest of the band sustained serious injuries but survived. Ironically, because of the plane's problems on an earlier flight, some members of the band had considered retiring it, and Cassie Gaines had been talked out of riding in the equipment truck only after repeated assurances of the plane's safety. Although it was presumed that fuel shortage was the cause of the crash, a lawsuit claiming mechanical negligence was filed against the airline company the following year.

MCA immediately withdrew *Street Survivors* due to its eerily prophetic cover photo of the band engulfed in flames and the enclosed order form for the Lynyrd Skynyrd Survival Kit. *Street Survivors* was reissued with a new cover and proved to be one of the band's biggest sellers, reaching platinum status. The surviving members of the band continued to record on and off for several years before finally splitting apart.

Allen Collins, always a party boy, had a change of heart in the mid-eighties after spending thirty days in jail for various drug charges. He declared that he had found God and joined a Christian band, but he was not rewarded for his conversion. Just days after his release from jail,

Collins and his girlfriend were driving home when their car ran off the road and crashed into a culvert. Allen was left paralyzed from the waist down and his girlfriend was killed. The car crash ended Collin's active life, and four years later, on January 23, 1990, he died of pneumonia in a Jacksonville, Florida, hospital.

The New York Dolls
Jerry Nolan, Billy Murcia, and Johnny Thunders

The New York Dolls will not go down in history as one of the great rock 'n' roll bands. Inspired by the Rolling Stones, the New York Dolls were unable to mimic their success because they lacked the Stones' skill and creativity. Ironically, the Dolls hold a place in rock 'n' roll history because of their very lack of greatness. Their unbelievable showmanship and flamboyance, and their onstage antics were accompanied by often unmelodic, rough-around-the-edges music. Others began to in turn imitate the Dolls, perhaps mistaking their amateurish performances for studied deconstructivism. It can be said that the New York Dolls, entrenched in their glam rock extravagance, paved the way for the minimalist punk movement which was embodied by the Sex Pistols.

By the end of the 1960's, the Rolling Stones were at the top of the rock 'n' roll world. They combined musical innovations with a wild reckless image that reflected the mind-set of their generation. Such greatness obviously begged for imitation, and the New York Dolls were among the first in line. David Johansen, the Dolls vocalist, fashioned himself after the strutting Mick Jagger. Johnny Thunders looked to Keith Richards for his role model, but both he and fellow guitarist Sylvain Sylvain could boast only of moderate raw talent and little technical skill. Arthur Kane on bass and

Jerry Nolan (replacing Billy Murcia) on drums were energetic and aggressive, but they lacked the polish and skill of Bill Wyman or Charlie Watts. What the New York Dolls wanted in musicality, they made up for in visual showmanship, and their androgynous flash aligned them with the growing glam rock scenes of New York and London. Glam rock was known for its fairly shallow approach to rock 'n' roll, and the Dolls were accordingly dismissed by most critics.

One man, however, was sure he saw and heard something behind the showy costumes and makeup. Todd Rundgren became the producer of the New York Dolls because he recognized the deconstructivist potential in their sound. The Dolls played loud crashing lines, and because Sylvain and Thunders did not have the skill to keep the violent jaggedness under control, the result came dangerously close to cacophony. The unrefined sound gained a hard-core following in New York but had, needless to say, little commercial appeal—in 1973 the New York Dolls' debut, an eponymous album, received virtually no attention from the general public.

The Dolls did not despair, and they followed their debut with a second flop entitled *Too Much Too Soon* in 1974. In spite of the two failures, the Dolls' following persevered, and some of the fans became musicians themselves. Many of these musician fans had, in fact, skill where the Dolls lacked it, and they were able to channel the rough-edged emotional music into a tight sound. The Ramones, for instance, used some of the New York Dolls' ap-

proaches, taking them to a higher level. The controlled chaos became a recognized technique, and punk was born, not more than two years later. No longer did music have to be pretty or even enjoyable, and for better or for worse, the New York Dolls played a part in the evolution. As for the band itself, the New York Dolls themselves parted ways soon after the release of the second album. Nolan and Thunders went on to form a similar and equally unsuccessful band known as the Heartbreakers.

The impact of the New York Dolls, then, was as a stepping-stone in the continuum of rock 'n' roll development. Given this environment, it is no surprise that the band members were familiar with drugs. Billy Murcia, the original drummer, was the first casualty. Heroin was his drug of choice, and not long before the Dolls began to record their debut album, Billy made the deadly mistake of supplementing his injections with a few too many drinks. Back in his London hotel room, Billy's girlfriend tried to revive him—but inexplicably did not consider the option of seeking medical aid. She walked him in circles around the hotel room. She soaked him in an ice-cold bathtub. She forced him to drink hot coffee. Ironically, it was the coffee that officially killed him—he choked on it. The death certificate cites "drowning" as the cause of death. Billy Murcia "drowned" on his black coffee at the age of twenty-one.

Another hotel room, this one in New Orleans, was the site of the next Doll death, in 1991. Johnny Thunders, né John Genzale, mixed alcohol with his drug of choice, which was methadone. He went to sleep and never woke up. He was thirty-eight years old.

The next year Jerry Nolan died of a stroke after undergoing treatment for pneumonia and meningitis. He was forty-five.

The Pretenders
James Honeyman-Scott and Peter Farndon

The Pretenders were one of the first bands to define the sound of the 1980's. Peter Farndon and James Honeyman-Scott embodied the eighties in another way as well—in their worship of excess.

Pete Farndon was born June 12, 1952, in the town of Hereford, England, near the Welsh border. Growing up he played bass in numerous bands and as a youth spent two years in Australia playing in a popular folk-rock band called the Bushwhackers. He traveled next to Hong Kong, where he experimented heavily with drugs before returning to Hereford in early 1978.

James Honeyman-Scott was born November 4, 1957, in Hereford and grew up with future band mate Farndon. Emulating heroes Jeff Beck and Eric Clapton, James began playing guitar in local bands at the age of eleven, worked in a music store at the age of thirteen, and left home at the age of fifteen. In 1973, he formed the band Cheeks with Hereford drummer Marin Chambers and keyboardist Verden Allen (of Mott the Hoople fame). The group toured for three years and then broke up, having never recorded.

Pete Farndon met American singer Chrissie Hynde in London in March of 1978 and they soon began to assemble a band, later adding old Hereford friend Honeyman-Scott and drummer Gerry Mackleduff. James was an exceptional guitarist and possessed an arranging skill which was crucial to the group's new sound. Chrissie's songwriting was an excellent complement to his agile style, and the team was in the studio by July. They recorded a three-song demo, consisting of Hynde compositions "Precious" and "The Wait" and a cover of the 1964 Kinks song "Stop Your Sobbing." In the fall, after hearing the tape, Nick Lowe offered to produce a single, which was recorded in one day during a break from his production of Elvis Costello's *Armed Forces* album.

Finally deciding on a name, the Pretenders immediately left for their debut performance at a weeklong booking in Paris. In December there were some interpersonal problems and Gerry Mackleduff was replaced by Martin Chambers (also from Hereford) and the band was soon signed by Real Records, a new label with distribution through WEA. In February 1979, the band made their UK chart debut as the first single "Stop Your Sobbing," reached number thirty-four. In July, the follow-up single "Kid" reached UK number thirty-three, which led to a monthlong sellout British tour, including dates at London's famed Marquee Club. The Pretenders released their third single, "Brass in Pocket," a Hynde/Honeyman-Scott composition that soared to UK number one. The band closed out the year with a December appearance at the all-star benefit "Concert for Kampuchea" at London's Hammersmith Odeon.

In January 1980, Real Records was bought by Sire and the new label released the Pretenders' eponymous debut album, an offering which hit the UK number one spot and rose to U.S. number nine. Promoting the album, the Pretenders toured extensively throughout Britain, Europe, and Japan, and by the time they began their first U.S. tour in April, the new single "Talk of the Town" was a

worldwide hit. November saw the band in Paris to start recording the next album, and they closed out the year by being named *Rolling Stone* magazine's Best New Artist.

With this critical as well as their commercial success, the Pretenders were in many ways the first major band of the eighties. A hectic schedule of touring and recording continued throughout early 1981, when the band released a five-song EP in the U.S. and the single "Message of Love" in England. In April, James took time out to marry American model Peggy Sue Fender in London. In August the album *Pretenders II* was released and the group embarked on a three-month U.S. tour, which was cut short when Martin Chambers sustained a thirty-stitch cut from a broken vase in a Philadelphia hotel room.

Both Pete and James had a difficult time adjusting to their success and frenzied lifestyle, and both turned to drugs for escape. Pete became especially dependent, and his heroin habits were the direct cause of declining musical skills. At the time, James' problem with cocaine was not thought to have been as severe as he strongly held his own as part of the band. The difficulties Pete presented for the band, however, eventually became intolerable. Personality clashes compounded the band's frustration with Pete's declining musicianship. The rift became insurmountable and on June 14, 1982, the Pretenders fired Pete Farndon.

James was shaken up by Pete's dismissal and he returned to London from an extended U.S. vacation, where he had played with the touring Beach Boys. A few days after his return, James attended a charity concert at the Venue, a local London club. Suffering from a cold, he drank only Perrier throughout the evening, then left to spend the night at the home of a friend. He went to sleep and never woke up. On June 16, 1982, James Honeyman-Scott was found dead, at the age of twenty-five. The Westminster Coroner's Court reported that although their autopsy findings were inconclusive, an overdose of cocaine was the probable cause of death.

The Pretenders continued on, and with fill-ins Tony Butler (Big Country) and Billy Bremner (Rockpile) released the single, "Back on the Chain Gang" in January of 1983. Dedicated to James, the song hit number five in the U.S. and was included on the soundtrack for the motion picture *The King of Comedy*.

During this time, Pete Farndon was in the process of forming a new band with Rob Stoner and ex-Clash member Topper Headon. The Pretenders were at the same time considering bringing him back, but Pete's lifestyle caught up with him before either could happen, and on April 14, 1983, less than a year after James' death, Pete Farndon's body gave out under the pressure of drugs. That night, Pete shot himself up with heroin and died of a drug-induced heart attack in the bathtub of his London house. James and Pete were both buried in their hometown of Hereford. Chrissie and Martin hired guitarist Robbie McIntosh (Manfred Mann's Earth Band) and bassist Malcolm Foster as permanent replacements for James and Pete. The new Pretenders debuted on May 28, 1983 at the US Festival in San Bernardino, California.

The Temptations
Eddie Kendricks, David Ruffin, and Paul Williams

The Temptations will go down in history as one of the most popular vocal groups of all time. Their close harmonies and satin presentation won them throngs of fans and critical acclaim for over two decades.

Eddie Kendricks (12/2/39) and Paul Williams (7/2/39) were born and raised in Birmingham, Alabama, and they formed their first group, the Cavaliers, while they were still in high school. Moving to Cleveland, then Detroit, the Cavaliers went through several changes; soon they were known as the Primes and had adopted a sister group, the Primettes (who would become the Supremes). In 1960, Eddie and Paul joined another group, the Elgins, and after signing with Motown and changing the name one more time, the Temptations were born.

After two failed singles, drummer Eldridge Bryant was replaced by David Ruffin, born January 18, 1941, in Meridian, Mississippi. The Temptations started working with writer/producer Smokey Robinson in 1964 and soon the team produced a national hit, "The Way You Do the Things You Do," with Eddie Kendricks on lead vocal. Their chart success continued and in March of 1965 "My Girl" hit number one and went gold. "My Girl" also had the distinction of being the first number-one hit by a male Motown group.

So began the Temptations' reign as one of the most popular male vocal groups of the sixties and much of the seventies. They had twenty-one top-twenty hits between 1964 and 1971 including "Get Ready," "Beauty Is Only Skin Deep" and "I Wish It Would Rain." In 1968, however, David announced that he wanted to change the group's name to David Ruffin and the Temptations and the rest of the group was not amused. David left in a cloud of ill will and was replaced by Dennis Edwards. With Eddie and Dennis now trading lead vocals just as Eddie and David had, the success resumed with "Can't Get Next to You," "Ball of Confusion," "Psychedelic Shack," and "TCB" with the Supremes. In 1971, "Just My Imagination (Running Away with Me)" became the Temptations' third number one hit and Eddie's final song with the group—he decided to go solo.

At the same time, Paul Williams also left the group, but his departure was under doctor's orders. Paul had a serious alcohol problem which had caused his health to deteriorate drastically, and in the early seventies he was also suffering from marital and financial strain. Paul's downward spiral continued until August 17, 1973, when Paul Williams was found shot dead in his car just two blocks from Motown's Detroit office. Although his death was ruled a suicide, many of his friends thought otherwise due to several suspicious circumstances. (He was wearing only underwear and had been shot in the left side of the head with his right hand.) Rumors of a mob connection circulated, but the ensuing investigation proved nothing. Many old Motown friends were on hand for the funeral when Paul Williams was buried at the Woodlawn Cemetery in Detroit.

Meanwhile, just a year after leaving the Temptations, David Ruffin released his first solo single, for Motown, and "My Whole World Ended the Moment You Left Me" was a big chart hit. David enjoyed a short-lived run of hits, including several duets with his brother Jimmy.

From 1973 to 1978, Eddie Kendricks had a series of R&B and pop hits that included three at number one—"Keep on Truckin'," "Boogie Down," and "Shoeshine Boy." Eddie's success as a solo artist proved to be as brief as David's, and in 1982 the two rejoined the Temptations. The reunited group recorded an album, appropriately titled *Reunion*, and embarked on a tour that included a tribute to Paul Williams. The success of the tour was not enough to keep the group together, however, and when it was over, the Temptations disbanded again. In 1985, Eddie and David joined with Hall and Oates to perform "My Girl" and "The Way You Do the Things You Do" at the grand reopening of the Apollo Theater. The show and following live album were both very successful and led to a gold record, Grammy nomination, and a blockbuster Live-Aid performance.

The collaborative rebound did not last, due in part to David's drug problems. David and Eddie reunited once more in 1987 as Ruffin and Kendricks, also performing with Dennis Edwards, another ex-Temptation. The hit or miss pattern continued, with revivals and breakups. The off-stage life was just as rocky, and David's ongoing drug problem led him to several arrests, convictions, and rehabilitations. On January 18, 1989, at the Waldorf-Astoria in New York, David and Eddie made their final appearance with the Temptations at the group's induction into the Rock 'n' Roll Hall of Fame. In 1990, David released his last record, *Hurt the One You Love*, followed by a Ruffin/Kendricks/Edwards European tour in early 1991.

While on tour, David remained drug-free, but when he returned to Philadelphia, he returned to the drug scene. On May 31, 1991, at eleven P.M.,

David collected thousands of dollars in cash and borrowed a limo to take him to a crack house where he snorted a huge amount of cocaine. At 2:46 A.M., the limo dropped him off at the emergency room entrance of the University of Pennsylvania Hospital. David Ruffin was pronounced dead at 3:55 A.M. Although the official cause of death was drug overdose, the police would not rule out foul play and the money that David had been carrying was never found.

David's funeral was financed by longtime fan Michael Jackson. The service was held on Monday, June 10, at New Bethel Baptist Church, with performances by Stevie Wonder, the Four Tops, Aretha Franklin, and the remaining Temptations, who sang "My Girl" to a tearful congregation. The church was filled beyond its capacity with over 2,500 mourners and crowds more outside. The throngs followed the funeral procession to Woodlawn Cemetery where David was laid to rest near fellow Temptation Paul.

On October 5, 1992, in his hometown of Birmingham, Eddie Kendricks lost his fight against lung cancer at the Baptist Medical Center-Princeton, where he had been hospitalized since September 25. Like so many former Motown stars, Eddie died with no insurance and unresolved lawsuits with Motown over old royalties. Old friend Bobby Womack came to the rescue by organizing several tribute concerts featuring Hall and Oates, Gladys Knight, Little Richard, and many others, raising over $25,000 for Eddie's family.

The Velvet Underground
Nico, Angus MacLise, and Sterling Morrison

The Velvet Underground was in many ways the alter ego of the San Francisco flower children and psychedelics. If the hippies sang in bright colors, the Velvet Underground sang in black, white, and drab gray. While the hippies sang of peace and love and hope, the Velvet Underground steeped their music in grim reality and urban angst. Although the Velvet Underground did not enjoy wide commercial success, their sound was vital to the evolution of later styles—punk, art rock, New Wave, and grunge.

Nico was born Christa Paffgen in Cologne, Germany, in 1940. Her first break came in 1959 when she landed a small roll in Fellini's *La Dolce Vita*. From her film debut, Nico embarked on a modeling career and then headed to the recording studio. Her debut single, "The Last Man," featured an impressive lineup, including Jimmy Page and Brian Jones, but still failed to attract significant attention. Undaunted by her inauspicious beginnings, Nico picked up and moved to New York City in 1966, determined to continue her music career. In her first month in the city, Nico made an important friend in Andy Warhol, appearing later that year in his *Chelsea Girls*. It was also through Warhol that Nico made the acquaintance of the fledgling rock band the Velvet Underground.

Andy Warhol had become the manager of the Velvet Underground in 1965 after spotting the struggling group in a New York nightclub. When Warhol took the reins, the group consisted of vocalist Lou Reed, John Cale playing the electric viola, Sterling Morrison on guitar, and drummer Angus MacLise. The band had been called the Primitives until they decided to borrow the name Velvet Underground from the title of a pornographic novel. Andy Warhol introduced the group to the underground art world, and they performed in his proto-performance art exhibit, "The Exploding Plastic Inevitable."

In 1966, Warhol introduced the group to Nico,

his latest protégée. He "suggested" that the Velvet Underground hire Nico as a vocalist, and Angus MacLise left in protest against Warhol's artistic control of the band. He was replaced by a dynamic female drummer, Maureen Tucker. The rest of the band, grateful for Warhol's patronage, welcomed Nico into the fold and the group entered the studio. The album, *The Velvet Underground and Nico*, was released in March 1967, with little reaction from the public or the critics. Lou Reed wrote the songs, with help from Morrison, and though it went largely unnoticed by his contemporaries, the sound that Reed created was groundbreaking. "Heroin" was perhaps the most notable, a song loaded with pain and aggression. The music in general was characterized by Nico's eerie and ethereal vocals and deconstructed simplicity of the guitar lines. The avant-garde sound built a small but dedicated following, and the art-rock artists like Roxy Music and Brian Eno, as well as the entire punk movement, would soon name Velvet Underground as a major influence on their evolution.

Nico was after immediate fame, not eventual respect, and when the first album flopped, she left the Velvet Underground (some say she was fired). She returned to the Warhol set and appeared again in *Chelsea Girls* in 1968, this time alongside some big names in the music industry. Bob Dylan, Jackson Browne, Tim Hardin, and Tim Buckley joined her as did former band mates Lou Reed and John Cale. The production failed to garner the recognition Nico sought, but she persisted and made several more solo recordings over the next few years. She collaborated several times with John Cale. In 1974 they released *The End* and the concert album *June 1st, 1974*, and in 1985 they tried again with *Camera Obscura*. Neither album took off, nor did her 1981 solo *Drama Exile*, which featured covers of David Bowie and Lou Reed compositions. As the years went on, Nico's renown diminished and she played at smaller and smaller venues. Always trying to play her latest creation, Nico was often pressured into playing oldies from the Velvet Underground album.

The Velvet Underground in its original state effectively dissolved after one post-Nico album, but Cale and Reed went on to pursue successful solo careers. Cale thrived in the art-rock scene. Reed turned initially toward the garish world of glam-rock with his producer David Bowie and then grew into a respected solo artist. After Cale and Reed left, the remaining members of the Velvet Underground continued to tour before officially calling it quits. When the band finally did fold, Sterling Morrison became a professor of English and Medieval studies at the University of Texas. He also continued to work on musical projects with Maureen Tucker and in 1994 was a featured performer with the Hudson Valley Philharmonic.

Neither Angus MacLise nor Nico was ever able to settle into a niche the way their former colleagues were. After he left the Velvet Underground, Angus retreated from society into a world of drugs and mysticism. He packed up and headed to India to live out his life, which was cut short in 1979 when he died in Nepal of malnutrition. Nico met her end in a similarly exotic setting. She faded from the rock scene in the second half of the eighties and retreated into a life of strict privacy. In search of solitude, Nico traveled to Ibiza, a Spanish island in the western Mediterranean, in 1988. On a beautiful morning, she took her bicycle out for a ride and never returned. She had fallen from the bicycle and died hours later from resulting brain hemorrhages.

On August 30, 1995, Sterling Morrison died of cancer in Poughkeepsie, New York. Two months after his death, the Velvet Underground was inducted into the Rock 'N' Roll Hall of Fame.

Acknowledgments

Special thanks to my family for believing in me, for supporting me, and for always being there.

Mary Lorenz Dietz, my mother—she taught me to be strong, to work hard, and to fight for what I believe in. One of the biggest influences in my life, she is someone I love, respect, and can't ever thank enough.

Evelyn Highlund—for all the stories you told, you showed me how to save the memories and pass them along.

Leif Lorenz—a truly talented dancer/choreographer and loyal brother, you showed me a whole other side of music and art. Plus you're a loving husband and dad to Patti, Colten, and Mackiernan.

Evanne Dietz—for being the "smart one" (sorry mom) and responsible even when it's a drag and for hanging out at Morrison's grave with me.

To the memory of my father, Manfred Lorenz.

Peter James—for the friendship, those wild rock 'n' roll years, and all that music trivia.

Casey McMakin—for the motivation, for giving me space, for sharing the good times as well as the bad, and for the love. You are a major part of this.

Moss—for your invaluable assistance when it was needed most; I couldn't have finished without you.

Ronnie Cook—for making me start writing, ready or not (guess I forgive you), and for getting me hooked up.

Laurens R. Schwartz—for this deal, your time, much advice, and for putting up with the craziness.

Suzie—for always keeping my job when I needed it.

Robert Matheu—for all the great photos.

Ann McMakin—for giving me a place to write.

Doc—well, you know what for.

The World Famous Double Down Saloon—my Vegas escape.

To Elizabeth Beier and Boulevard (for this book), Lee Childers (remember way back when this started as a game), Eric (thanks for the typing and stuff), JJ (for all the computer help), Mick Schneider (for taxes and accountant stuff), Kurt and Vicki, Ducky Dietz, and for Giles's memory.

So many friends, lovers, relatives, co-workers, and others have passed through my life. You have inspired me, helped me, and believed in this. I just want to thank you for everything and I'm sorry if I missed any names: Candy, Jonathon, Lori, William, Liz, Brandon, Max, Michael, Helen, Paul, Mark, Brian Setzer (sorry Louis didn't make it), Jet, Sherry, Eric, Richard, Patti, Mimi and Sandy, John, Jeff, Dave Navarro, Lupe, Chris, Bobby, Elwin, Susan, Emma, Kathy, Matt, Al, Tony, Sara, Terry, Michelle, Toledo, Sean, Scott, Douglas, Jeannie, Gary, Chip, Katy, Dan, Jill, Karen, Andrea, Mona, Jenni, Aram, Patrick, Vicki, Bob, Lio, Lisa, Russ, Geraldine, Joey, Ron and Valerie, John and Yta, Biff, Kenny, Whitney, Jerry, Donnie, Rachel, Carlos, Don, Nancy, Morales, Tom and Ryan, Carl, Robert, all of The Corvettes, Russell, Tina, Darin.

I tried to keep it true and real for all the fans because that's what I'll always be.

Author Nikki Corvette is a Singer/Songwriter, formerly of Nikki and the Corvettes.